Odd and Unusual Tales From The Old West

By Alton Pryor

Odd and Unusual Tales From The Old West

By Alton Pryor

Stagecoach Publishing
5360 Campcreek Loop
Roseville, CA 95747
916-771-8166
stagecoach@surewest.net
www.stagecoachpublishing.com

Odd and Unusual Tales From The Old West

Copyright © Pryor 2006

ISBN: 0-9747551-3-3

Library of Congress Control Number: 2006906426

Stagecoach Publishing
5360 Campcreek Loop
Roseville, California
(916) 771-8166
stagecoach@surewest.net
www.stagecoachpublishing.net

*This book is dedicated to
the most beautiful girl in the
world, my granddaughter,*
Sarah Pearl Pryor
(Born May 16, 2006)

A Matter of Interpretation

Sitting Bull was a guest of honor at the opening ceremonies for the Northern Pacific Railroad. When it came his turn to speak, he said, in *Lakota* language, "I hate all white people. You are thieves and liars. You have taken away our land and made us outcasts."

A quick-thinking interpreter told the crowd the chief was happy to be there and that he looked forward to peace and prosperity with the white people.

Sitting bull received a standing ovation.

Table of Contents

Chapter 1

Seven Little Indians

They drew straws to see who would kill the babies.

It was a fall day at an Indian encampment in the Tonto Basin of Arizona. Lined up on their cradleboards against a rock wall were seven little Apache babies. The weather was so nice, some babies slept while others gazed out upon the strange world around them.

The late Roscoe G. Willson, in his Arizona Tales run regularly by *The Arizona Republic* newspaper, told this story. The story illustrated how otherwise hard-bitten men could not overcome the power that emanates from a baby.

All about the camp, in 1871, there was a scene of great activity. The men in the Apache camp came dashing in at early morn, driving a large herd of horses, stolen that very morning from the Bowers Ranch east of Prescott, Arizona.

The Apache men and women of the camp were excited as they talked about their great success. The women busied themselves cooking the meat of a horse they had slaughtered. They laid strips of raw horseflesh on the oak bushes to dry while they cooked the larger portion of horsemeat over an open fire.

When the meat was cooked, the men gorged themselves on the sweet horseflesh, which they favored above all other. When the men finished, the women too, then ate with gusto.

After tending and nursing their babies, the cherubs were returned to their papoose baskets along the wall. The women joined the group of men sleeping off their heavy meal beneath the deep shade of oak trees.

Soon, a clattering of blue jays signaled to the Indians that something was amiss. Before the Indians could rise to their feet, rifle shots rang out from the hillsides and oak thickets. Several Apache men and women were killed before they could rise.

The attackers were settlers from Prescott, on the hunt for the horses stolen that morning from the Bowers Ranch. John B. Townsend, an Indian fighter, headed the group. The Indians knew him to be brave and fearless and held him in great respect.

It wasn't until after the last Apache had either escaped, disappeared, or been killed that the seven little Indian babies were discovered resting against the wall.

This presented a problem for the rugged white men. In their attacks on settlers, the Apache Indians didn't hesitate to kill white women and children.

Captain Townsend looked at the babies snuggled in their papoose baskets. He scratched his head, knowing that usually the babies should be killed. But Townsend shuddered at the thought. "Good God," he asked himself, who could kill a baby in cold blood?"

Others in the party felt the babies should be killed, but the only question was, who would do the job.

Townsend decided the issue by saying they would draw straws to see who would commit the horrendous deed. Grass stems of different lengths were drawn. Townsend held the short straw.

When he pulled his pistol and stepped toward the nearest infant, the baby gurgled, wrinkled its face and smiled back at him. John's only vision at that point was a picture of his own baby girl back at his Agua Fria Ranch.

His pistol hand dropped to his side. He turned to his companions and murmured, "I just can't do it boys. Some one else will have go through with this."

Ed Wright, John's neighbor on the Agua Fria, stepped forward. "Boys, we can't any of us kill those babies I don't care if the Apaches have killed some of our children. We weren't raised like these Indians, and we'd all feel like murderers if we cold-bloodedly killed the little varmints. Let's leave 'em where they are and go make camp."

A sigh of relief sounded through the crowd. After making camp that evening, Ed Wright and some of the others used rawhide rope to lash the seven baby baskets high enough off the ground to be safe from coyotes or other varmints.

The next morning, the babies and their cradles were gone.

Chapter 2

The Tommyknockers

Gold miners were a superstitious lot, but none were more superstitious than the Cornish miners. The Cornish belief that certain supernatural powers protected their efforts was heartfelt and real. Belief can be a powerful force, even making you see things that don't exist. When the hard-rock miners went underground, they believed wholeheartedly that underground elves existed.

These elves were called *Tommyknockers.*

In a 1989 issue of Sierra Heritage Magazine, Gary Noy writes about the Tommyknockers.

Even though the Cornish were superstitious, they were the most sought after hard rock mining workers. Centuries of labor in the tin mines of Cornwall, England, gave these hardy workers a vast knowledge of tunneling and other mining techniques.

This knowledge, Noy writes, was perfectly suited to the mines of northern California. Along with these skills, the Cornish brought their colorful language, festive personalities, ironic view of life, and mining superstitions.

Cornish miners, considered the greatest miners in the world, were brought in to California to check the tunnel work of the Chinese by having them work in separate tunnels at the same time the Chinese were working. The Chinese, without fail, would cut more rock in a week than the Cornish miners did. The Cornish men left in disgust, saying they would no longer work with the Chinese.   (Bancroft Library)

The Cornish miner approached the dirty and dangerous task of hard-rock mining with irony, and with good cheer. One Cornish miner, when asked how to find a rich pocket of gold, replied, "Well, where gold is, it is, and where it hain't, there be I."

These Cornish miners imported their Tommyknockers to the Gold Country.

Tommyknockers were said to be direct descendants of ancient elves known as *Vugs* and *Piskies*. After emigrating to the Gold Country, the elves became Americanized and grew to be as important to the miner as his tin lunchbox, his hard hat, carbide lamp, and double jack.

Many Cornish miners refused to enter a mine until assured that tommyknockers were on duty, providing warnings, and helpful directions.

According to stories handed down from generation to generation, there were two kinds of tommyknockers that inhabited the mine—the friendly, helpful elf, and the mischievous nuisance elf.

Both are described as being little men about two feet high, dressed in miniature mining attire, complete with tiny picks, hard hats, and lunch buckets.

Germans call the elves *Berggeister* or *Bergmanniein.* This means 'ghosts" or "little miners". They watch over the earth's precious ores and metals.

The elves that befriended the miners also watched over the miners' children. More important, they worked alongside the miners deep in the mines. The elves led miners to rich ore veins, tested shaft conditions, pried down loose rocks, and issued life-saving warnings about cave-ins, water leaks,

19

and runaway carts by tapping on air pipes or timber supports.

Miners could readily recall times when tommyknockers saved their lives.

Frank Crampton, writing about tommyknockers in his book, *Deep Enough*, insists that the little elves saved his life.

Crampton had just squeezed into a tiny underground crawl space to load sticks of dynamite for blasting. He carefully placed the dynamite, lit the fuse, and then, according to Crampton, "The Tommyknockers began to raise hell," making all kinds of warning noises.

Instead of crawling out of the hole carefully, Crampton put on a head of steam to extract himself. As he exited the area, the whole thing blasted to pieces.

"I was lucky to get off with a few cuts and bruises from flying rock," he wrote. "I owed my life to the tommyknockers, these unseen, wee, small folk."

In another mining incident, this one at the Empire Mine in Grass Valley, California, a massive cave-in collapsed hundreds of feet of tunnel and caused extensive flooding—all during a shift change.

The miners firmly believed that tommyknockers held up the rock until the crew got out, and then released it. As was their common practice, the miners expressed their belief to the mine management.

In a 1957 interview in the *Sacramento Bee*, retired miner Fred Nettell, a member of a Grass

20

Valley Cornish family, described the miners attitude toward tommyknockers.

"When a Cornish miner of the old school tells you how his life was saved by a tommyknocker's warning, he is not being facetious. His respect and feeling toward these underground elves is almost religious."

When the tommyknockers are bad, they are believed to hurt miners who doubt their power or do not believe in them. They can also bring misery, fear and death when they are mad. Earthquakes were once believed to be their handiwork.

Chapter 3

Tombstone

Prospectors arrived in Arizona to prospect for gold and silver. One who struck it rich was Ed Schieffelin, who founded Tombstone, Arizona.   (Arizona State Historical Society)

Ed Schieffelin came to Arizona in 1877, where he took a job as an army scout at Fort Hauchuca. Ed was a prospector, on the constant prowl for the "big strike". In Arizona, he first prospected in the Grand Canyon area without much luck.

Working as a scout at Fort Hauchuca, Arizona, Ed, in his spare time, kept an eye out for potential prospecting sites. When he ventured into Apache country to search for silver, soldiers at the fort joshed him about his rock collecting.

"The only rock you will find out there will be your tombstone," they told him.

Ed discovered several successful silver mines in the area. He decided to call his first and most successful mine "Tombstone", reminiscent of the warnings his friends gave him about prospecting in Apache country.

Ed Schieffelin

The town of Tombstone, Arizona was thus born as it sprang up around Ed Schieffelin's silver mines.

When Tombstone's mines exhausted their silver in the late 1880s, Ed Schieffelin was a rich man. He left Tombstone and traveled the country, prospecting for a while in Alaska and also in Oregon.

Schieffelin died at age 49 of natural causes while prospecting in Oregon. He was found alone in a miner's cabin, slumped over valuable samples of ore, the origin of which was unknown. In his journal he had written, "Struck it rich again, by God."

As requested in his will, Schieffelin is interred two miles from Tombstone (at a cemetery located at West Allen Street). As specified in his will, he was buried in mining clothes with a pick, shovel and his old canteen.

Tombstone was a wild town. Lawlessness and violence became such a problem in Tombstone's hey-day that President Chester A. Arthur threatened to declare martial law in the town.

A legend of Tombstone's early days is the now famous "Gunfight at the O.K. Corral", much of which has been fictionalized beyond its original occurrence.

Many claim that the Earp brothers, along with their friend, Doc. Holladay, provoked the "shootout".

Rustlers, horse thieves, and desperados terrorized Southeastern Arizona at the time. These outlaws were loosely termed the "Cowboy Element". The best known of this "Cowboy Element' was the Clanton Clan, led by N.C. "Old Man" Clanton.

The Clanton family included sons Peter, Joseph Isaac (Ike), Phineas (Phin) and Billy, the youngest and still a teenager. Joining the Clantons in their clandestine operations were the McLaury brothers, Tom and Frank.

25

Ed Schieffelin is shown seated at the right in the days after silver brought him prosperity. His younger brother Eff is seated across from him. Others in the picture are not identified. (Bank of Douglas)

Soon after he arrived in Tombstone, Wyatt Earp was appointed deputy sheriff.

There was bad blood between the Clantons and the Earp brothers from the beginning. Both sides verbally threatened each other. Virgil Earp, a deputy U.S. Marshall, became embroiled in physical arguments with the McLaurys and Ike Clanton.

Doc Holliday entered the picture at this time. Doc was a dentist by trade, but in the west he was a professional gambler and a close friend of the Earp brothers. Some say it was Doc that was the real source of the trouble between the Earps and the Clanton gang.

During one evening in the Alhambra Saloon, Ike Clanton was drunk and began making threats against the Earps and Doc Holliday. When Doc heard of the threats, he entered the saloon and tried to provoke Clanton into drawing his gun. Ike, however, wasn't armed, as Tombstone had an ordinance against being armed while in town.

Holliday then tried to talk a saloon patron into getting Ike a gun. Morgan Earp entered the saloon and broke up the argument between Holliday and Clanton. Even so, the fight continued into the street.

Ike Clanton spotted Wyatt Earp, and boasted that he would have him "man for man" the next day. Instead of going to bed, the young Clanton gambled all night, some say in a game that included Sheriff John Behan and City Marshal Virgil Earp.

27

Clanton was still mouthing threats and carrying a rifle through town the next morning, shouting he would shoot the first Earp that he saw. Virgil Earp, in his position as marshal decided to haul Clanton to jail, charging him with violating the town ordinance against carrying firearms.

The court fined Clanton $25 and ordered him to surrender his rifle, leaving him unarmed. The young outlaw still continued his threat to get even with the Earps.

Wyatt gave what is now his famous response: "If you are so anxious to make a fight, I will go anywhere on earth to make a fight with you."

On October 26, 1881, the Clantons and McLaurys were at the O.K. Corral. They planned to get their horses and head home, but at the same time, they were still making threats against the Earps.

Word got back to Marshal Virgil Earp, who then decided to deputize Doc Holliday. This meant that every man in the Earp party was now a lawman.

Despite the legend, no shooting actually took place at the O.K. Corral. As the Earps and Doc made their way through town, they passed the O.K. Corral, but the Clantons and McLaurys were not there. They were waiting in the alley by Fly's Photo Shop.

When they were spotted by Virgil, he told them, "Throw up your hands. I have come to disarm you."

According to witnesses, Billy Clanton said, "Don't shoot me. I don't want to fight."

Tom McLaury opened his coat, showing that he too, was unarmed. Ike Clanton ran up to Wyatt, but no one knows for sure who fired first.

Wyatt Earp gave this account:

> *I knew that Frank McLaury had the reputation of being a good shot and a dangerous man, and I aimed at Frank McLaury...My first shot struck Frank McLaury in the belly...If Tom McLaury was unarmed I did not know it.*

Sheriff John Behan, who saw the shootout, gave this version:

> *...the first man that I was certain was hit was Frank McLaury, as I saw him staggering and bewildered and knew he was hit...Ike Clanton broke and ran after the first few shots were fired; Ike, I think, went through Fly's Building; the last I saw of him he was running through the back of Fly's Building toward Allen Street.*

R.J. Coleman, who also witnessed the event, gave this account:

> *Billy Clanton stood in the same position I first saw him; I saw him fire two or three shots in a crouched position; one of them hit Morgan Earp, who stumbled or fell, he jumped up*

again and commenced shooting...I think Billy Clanton must have been struck, but was down in a crouching position, and using the pistol across his knee and fired two shots, one of which hit Marshal (Virgil) Earp; Wyatt and Morgan were still firing at him, when he raised himself up and then fell, still holding his pistol in his hand.

Billy Clanton, Tom and Frank McLaury soon died. The only armed person without injury was Wyatt Earp. Sheriff Behan arrested Wyatt for murder. Three days after the shoot-out, the coroner held an inquest. The Earps moved into the Cosmopolitan Hotel, which was deemed to be safer for them than their own homes.

Several witnesses, including Sheriff Behan and Ike Clanton testified at the inquest. At the conclusion of the inquest, the ten jurors found:

...After viewing the body and hearing such testimony as had been submitted to us, find that the person was Frank McLaury...and that he came to his death in the town of Tombstone in said county, and on the 26th day of October, 1881, from the effects of pistol and gunshot wounds inflicted by Virgil Earp, Morgan Earp, Wyatt Earp and one Holliday, commonly called Doc Holliday.

...The verdict in the case of William Clanton and Thomas McLaury was the same as above.

Wyatt asked that he not be arrested on the day of the shooting so that he could attend to his wounded brothers. On November 4, 1881, Wyatt, along with Doc Holliday, was arrested and charged with the murders of the McLaurys and Billy Clanton.

It was fortunate for Wyatt that his friend, Wells Spicer, was the presiding judge. The judge allowed Wyatt to testify by reading a statement prepared by his lawyer. The defense lawyers had no cross-examination.

Among the dozen witnesses was H.F. Sills, a railroad engineer who testified he heard the Clantons and McLaurys say they were going to "kill Virgil Earp."

To Judge Spicer, facts about Ike Clanton were the most important. His taunting threats had started the whole affair, but Clanton was not injured at all. Part of Judge Spicer's opinion, issued December 1, 1881, follows:

...the great fact, most prominent in the matter, to wit, that Isaac Clanton was not injured at all, and could have been killed first and easiest...I...cannot resist firm conviction that the Earps acted wisely, discreetly, and prudentially to secure their own self preservation—they saw at once the

dire necessity of giving the first shot to save themselves from certain death...it was a necessary act done in the discharge of official duty.

The story didn't end there. Judge Spicer received a threat that he would be assassinated. (He wasn't.) On December 28, 1881, Virgil Earp, who was still marshal, was shot in the left arm while crossing the street. He was unable to use his left arm again.

The next month, Morgan Earp was playing billiards in a Tombstone saloon when he was shot in the back. He died from the gunshot. Another bullet narrowly missed Wyatt.

Wyatt killed the man who shot his brother.

The famous gunfight at the O.K. Corral was over in twenty or thirty seconds, according to Sheriff Behan. The countless versions depicting the battle in movies, television and radio documentaries were not only exaggerated, but distorted and greatly fictionalized.

Chapter 4

The Lost Adams Diggings

'A gold story that may really be true'

Somewhere out there in a deep trough-like box canyon a small creek flows. There lies the Lost Adams Diggings, as rich as any of the lost treasures of the west, and perhaps the most legitimate in terms of factual evidence. It is a tale corroborated by more than one individual.

The man named Adams was a teamster on his way to Los Angeles with 12 horses. Adams (his first name was variously given as William, Edward, Henry and John) was an overland freighter, hauling goods for a price, between Los Angeles and Tucson, Arizona. He was married, with a wife and three children in Los Angeles.

Is this a lost gold mine?
(Google Images)

After his last trip, Adams camped in the vicinity of Florence, Arizona. Apaches, making off with his

33

horses, awakened him. Adams gave chase and recovered the animals.

When he returned to his encampment, he found his wagon burning and all of his other goods, including the two thousand dollars received from his freight delivery, were gone. The Apache's had simply used the *horse-stealing* ploy to allow them to plunder the camp of its real valuables.

With his valuables gone, save for the 12 horses, the penniless Adams went to a friendly Pima Indian village at what is now Gila Bend, Arizona. There he listened to miners trade stories about prospecting. A half-breed Mexican-Apache nicknamed "Gotch Ear" listened as the miners voiced their desires to find gold. The lad was called Gotch Ear because of a deformed and crumpled lobe of one ear.

Apaches captured Gotch Ear and his brother when they were young boys living in Mexico. Gotch Ear was now on the run from the tribe because he killed the Apache who killed his brother in a fight.

Gotch Ear finally approached miner group. If you're interested in gold, he told them, he knew of a canyon ten days away on horseback, where a creek literally flowed with gold nuggets. All he asked in return was a horse that would take him back to Mexico.

It was in 1864 that Gotch Ear guided the group of 22 men to the site. Gotch Ear led the gold-lusting group down the Gila River in a general northeast direction for several days. On or about August 25, the group camped in the low area between two lofty peaks, believed to be Mt. Ord and Mt. Baldy.

This has led to confusion for treasure seekers, however, as Mount Ord is located north of Phoenix and is wrong for the journey taken by Gotch Ear and his followers.

Since Adams had all the horses, the gold-hungry miners chose him as their leader.

After four days of travel through heavy timber, the Mexican youth led the miners around a high mountain which Adams and John Brewer, another one of the miners, say was the White Mountains of eastern Arizona.

The group finally reached what appeared to be a box canyon. Here they camped for the night. In the morning, they rode up the canyon toward a reddish-colored bluff, but which was really a solid rock wall sixty to seventy feet high.

Gotch Ear led the men around a huge boulder at the base of the wall. There, through a hidden portal, they went into a zigzag canyon, so tight Adams said later, that a rider stretching his arms wide could touch both sides.

Running along the floor of the canyon was a stream, which they followed to an acre-sized meadow. Here they made camp for the night.

The miners had hardly settled and began gathering the yellow metal before a band of Apaches, led by Chief Nana, appeared in the meadow near a waterfall.

Nana told the miners to take what they wanted from the creek, but to make no effort to locate the gold deposits further up the canyon above the waterfall. He also ordered them to leave soon, and never return.

"Gotch Ear" led the gold seekers to a box canyon.

(Google Images)

While the gold held no allure for the Indians, the canyon where it was located did. The canyon, called "Sno-Tah-Hay" by Nana, was a very special religious site for the Indians.

The Apaches also believed that gold was the "tears of the sun". Nobody touched the tears of the sun because it was the source of all life.

The gold seekers remained in the canyon against the orders of Nana. Not only did they stay, but soon began construction on a cabin. In three weeks time, they had accumulated about sixty thousand dollars worth of gold, which they placed in a container and hid in the hearth of the unfinished cabin.

The intent was to later distribute the gold evenly to the men in the prospecting party, with the exception of a German named Snively. Snively took his share each day and kept his gold apart from the others.

Supplies soon ran low. A party of five miners, led by John Brewer, was assigned to go to Fort Wingate to restock the camp. The miners carried with them nuggets—some as big as turkey eggs—to use as payment.

At the fort, when the miners paid for their supplies with the huge gold nuggets, the storekeeper carefully noted this fact.

Meanwhile, the Apache Chief Nana, unseen, continued watching the activity at the creek, and also noted the surreptitious nighttime trips up the canyon to seek the source of the gold.

He was not pleased. He ordered his Apache warriors to kill the five-man supply group as it returned from Fort Wingate. This was done with the exception of one man, Brewer, who escaped.

The Apaches then killed all the miners in the canyon except for two men who were a distance away from the Anglo encampment. Snively, the German, who had already taken his gold and returned to Germany. Years later, Snively verified in detail the existence of the gold.

One of the two men who escaped the Apache massacre was Adams, and the other was Jack Davidson. The only reason the two men escaped the Apache wrath is they had gone in search of the long overdue Fort Wingate supply crew.

Adams and Davidson decided for safety it was best to head for Los Angeles to avoid further contact with the Apaches. Traveling at night, they became lost.

They were spotted by U.S. soldiers and taken to Fort Apache, according to one story. This casts some doubt on this version, however, as Fort Apache was not established until 1872.

Jack Davidson later claimed they were taken to Fort Whipple, east of Prescott.

Adams and Davidson did not know that John Brewer, who headed the supply party, had also escaped the Apache massacre. Brewer climbed up the canyon wall and reached friendly Pueblo Indians. Brewer eventually went to Colorado, married an Indian woman and raised a family.

Adams returned to his family in California and remained there for ten years. He was afraid to return to New Mexico to look for the diggings.

Adams did return in 1874. He searched and searched for the lost "Adams Diggings" until his death in 1876, but was never able to relocate the gold mine.

There are stories galore about attempts to retrace the path taken by Gotch Ear and his Anglo followers.

A man named Edward Doheny, traveling across New Mexico into Phoenix looking for a job, reported he had traveled down a box canyon before he realized he could not cross it. He noticed the ruins of a burned-out cabin before turning back, but, at the time, he knew nothing of the Adams story.

When later grubstaked, Doheny was unable to find the location again.

A cowboy named Jack Townsend claimed to have found the site of the Lost Adams Diggings in New Mexico in 1894, while working out of Magdalena, New Mexico. This was never confirmed.

Once, during the period when he was trying to relocate the "gold river", Adams met a Bob Lewis in a saloon. Lewis, too, had been searching for the "Diggings".

"Go and look for the bones of those men who were carrying supplies in the canyon. Show me the bones, and I'll show you the gold."

According to an account by Lee Paul, on a website called "The Outlaws," Lewis did find the bones. He found them thirty years later. Stacked into a crevice were the skeletons of several men covered with pieces of packsaddles and rocks.

Lewis was in the Datil Mountains of New Mexico. While he found the bones, he could not find the secret door. It is believed that an earthquake, which shook southern Arizona and New Mexico in 1887, had rearranged the scenery in the Datil Mountains.

Many, many efforts have been made to trace the path laid out by Gotch Ear. None have proved fruitful. It seems The Lost Adams Diggings will remain just that—lost.

Chapter 5

Sand Dune Whiskey Cache

This tale cannot help but intrigue the treasure hunter. It concerns a freighter transporting a load of one hundred proof whiskeys that was one hundred-twenty-two-years old from California to northern Arizona mining camps.

The route of the teamster has not been ascertained, but it is known that he encountered a vicious sandstorm. The loss occurred somewhere between eighteen and twenty-three miles south of Beatty, Nevada. Beatty is located in southern Nye County at the sand dunes.

When confronted by the sandstorm, the freight hauler hobbled his team and took refuge under his wagonload of whiskey. When the skies cleared the following day, the team had drifted away and left no tracks to follow.

Stowing all the water he could carry in a backpack, the freighter set out on foot for the same ranch he had just left in the Oasis Valley. The trip took him a day-and-a-half on foot.

He borrowed a hitch of draft horses to use in recovering his wagonload of whiskey. When the unnamed freighter returned to the site where his wagon and load of whiskey should have been, there was nothing there.

It is concluded that another sandstorm had shifted the huge dunes, covering the wagon and its cargo. The teamster then returned the borrowed horses to the Oasis Valley ranch.

The sand dunes of the Arizona, California and Nevada desert can be incredible, eerie, treacherous and inhospitable forces of nature. There are some reports that small anthills form the nucleus upon which some sand dunes are built.

Some California dunes with crests only 30 feet high may advance fifty feet a year, posing a serious threat to nearby farms and roads.

The shifting sand dunes of the desert.
(Google Images)

There are several discrepancies to the tale of the freighter and his load of whiskey. For one thing, Oasis Valley is about 100-miles to the northwest of the sand dunes and the freighter could not have walked the distance in a day-and-a-half.

Another thing that doesn't quite jibe is that in the 1880s, freight shipped from northern California to northern Arizona was routed through central California by rail to Needles, California and Kingman, Arizona.

Some desert residents believe the freighter stopped at Rose's Well, a then-active stage station some 18-miles south of Beatty.

Another tale out of Nye County is that of a gambler. This gambler, in what is now the ghost town of Tybo, cleaned the miners out of about three thousand dollars in gold coins during a wild poker game.

It wasn't long before a rumor circulated that the gambler had used a marked deck. The livid miners planned to jump the gambler and retrieve their losses.

Hearing the rumor, the gambler boarded the Belmont stage. A short distance out of Tybo, the gambler stopped the driver while he walked into the sagebrush with his money in a canvas sack.

When he returned to the stage, he no longer had the canvas sack. He told the driver he would return for it after things had cooled down a bit.

Three days later, the gambler was killed in a gunfight in the Belmont Saloon. His canvas sack of gold coins may still lie in the desert a short distance east of Tybo.

Chapter 6

Passing of the Telegram

It is likely that most young people don't even know what the term *telegram* means, let alone having sent or received one.

The telegram passed without a retirement party. It just went. Not even a small announcement was made by Western Union.

It should be noted that it was the telegraph that put the Pony Express out of business, much like the coming of the railroads did to the Santa Fe and Oregon Trails.

Samuel Morse invented the telegraph in 1831. (Google Images)

The telegraph changed the world when inventor Samuel Morse sent those fateful first words, "What hath God wrought" on May 24, 1844 from Washington, D.C. to Baltimore. Morse sent the message to his assistant, Alfred Vail.

Morse found it difficult to convince the public that his new invention was anything more than a "curiosity".

While a professor at New York University, Morse proved in 1835 that signals could be transmitted by wire and produce written codes on paper. When he modified the system to write dots and dashes, the public remained skeptical.

This painting was considered a symbol of unabashed American expansionism. *Manifest Destiny,* painted by John Gast, moves steadily westward stringing telegraph wires, with settlers and miners in her wake.   (Library of Congress)

When the economy was on an upturn, Morse asked Congress to appropriate funds to build a telegraph line from Washington to Baltimore, forty miles away. He received a $30,000 grant to build his line February 23, 1843.

His historic "What hath God wrought" message was sent May 24, 1844. Still, the government balked at purchasing Morse's invention. It was left to private enterprise to develop the expansion of the telegraph.

By 1856, thirty or forty rival companies were working on different patents of the telegraph. The New York and Mississippi Valley Printing Telegraph Company, formed in 1851, walked into the melee, buying up several rival companies.

The firm changed its name to Western Union Telegraph Company. It completed the first transcontinental telegraph line five years later, putting Pony Express out of business.

Even though the telephone technology advanced rapidly, long distance phone calls remained expensive, and the use of telegrams peaked during the 1920s and 30s when it was cheaper to send a wire than it was to call by phone.

Morse's assistant Alfred Vail invented this "finger key".
(Google Images)

During World War II, the War Department used Western Union to notify families of deaths and injuries to armed forces personnel. Western Union couriers became a feared sight for some people who had relatives in the military.

Western Union phased out its couriers in the 1960s and early 70s when faxes, email and long distance rates improved. By 2005, only 20,000 telegrams were sent worldwide.

Morse and His Code

In 1836, Samuel Morse demonstrated the ability to transmit information over wires. This information was sent as a series of electrical signals. Short signals were referred to as *dits,* while longer signals were called *dahs.*

A . would represent a dit, while a dash – represented a dah. The telegraph code's most well-known use is for the distress signal: SOS. The SOS signal is sent as:

S   O   S
... - - - ...

Morse code relies on precise intervals of time between dits and dahs, between letters, and between words.

dit	1 unit of time
dah	3 units of time
pause between letters	3 units of time
pause between words	7 units of time

The speed of transmitting Morse code is measured in wpm (words per minute). The word "Paris" is used as the standard length of a word.

To transmit the word "Paris" requires 50 units of time. If you transmitted the word "Paris" five times, you would be transmitting at 5 wpm. An experienced operator could transmit and receive information at 20 to 30 wpm.

Chapter 7

Lost Treasure of Mission San Miguel

It was a period of poor times for California's missions, and more especially so for Mission San Miguel.

Mission San Miguel never ranked with the best of the missions.

Founded in 1797 by Father Fermin Lausuen, the mission, located in San Luis Obispo County, was named for "Saint Michael, Captain of the Armies of God". The mission completed the northern half of the mission chain from San Luis Obispo to San Francisco.

By 1803, there were more than 1,000 neophytes there. By 1805, there were several adobe houses and forty-seven Indian houses there as well.

A serious fire destroyed most of the San Miguel mission buildings in 1806, but help poured in from other missions to restore them.

The natives found San Miguel Mission a haven. The mission was one of the last to be secularized and turned over to civil authorities in 1836. At this time, most of the natives either left or ran away, and three years after secularization, the mission buildings were in such poor condition that Father Moreno and Father Abello were forced to leave.

Courtyard of Mission San Miguel today. (Google Images)

Governor Pio Pico sold the land and buildings to Petronio Rios and an Englishman named William Reed in 1846 for six hundred dollars. (There are some reports that the sale was for a mere two hundred fifty dollars.)

Reed and Rios then decided to try their hand at prospecting and headed for the mines. The pair did moderately well at the placers, but by no means to the extent that Reed had hoped.

Unfortunately, the foolish young Reed was given to braggadocio, implying to those around him in a bar that they had indeed struck it rich.

The older and more sensible Petronio did not like him talking so loose. "Here we are," Rios would say, "among all kinds of wild fellows, and it is not wise to make all this talk of the money we are supposed to have. We are in danger of losing the little we have made."

Tiring of the mines, Reed returned to his sheep and cattle at San Miguel, while Rios settled in Templeton, just south of Paso Robles. Reed oversaw both his own and Rios' livestock at the mission. The mission was quiet and lonely, save for the presence of Reed and his family.

Reed used the mission as his home and soon opened a store there. It became a stopping place for miners traveling from Los Angeles to San Francisco during the gold rush.

Reed insisted that travelers pay for rooms and meals in gold. He charged exorbitant rates in both his store and in the inn and boasted of accumulating a fortune from the travelers.

There were no banks to deposit his wealth. He therefore felt the only thing to do was to bury the gold coins.

The granddaughter of Petronio, Reed's partner, tells the grisly details of what happened when five suspicious travelers stopped at the inn one night.

"One evening a party of men came to the mission. There were three Americans, an Irishman, and an Indian who acted as a guide. The white men had known Mr. Reed at the mines, and

53

he welcomed them accordingly. Still he kept up the pretence of having made lots of money at the mines."

During the evening, the men admitted stealing five horses in Monterey before coming to Reed's mission inn. Concerned they may have been followed by lawmen, the five men became noticeably nervous.

When one man went to check on the horses, another noticed the heavy leather pouch attached to Reed's belt. Reed admitted to the outlaw that the pouch contained gold coins.

When he inquired about the coins, Reed, whose tongue was loosened by the wine and alcohol consumed earlier, admitted to burying thousands of dollars in a secret location behind the headquarters.

One of the men pulled a long dagger from beneath his coat and held it to Reed's throat. He demanded to know exactly where the coins were buried.

Reed cursed the man, who then plunged the dagger into the innkeeper's throat, instantly killing him. The outlaws rounded up Reed's wife and two children. When they professed no knowledge of where the gold was buried, they, too, were killed.

Servants were questioned in turn. As they claimed ignorance of any buried treasure, they joined the growing number of those killed. In all, thirteen people became victims of the enraged killers.

The men dug up the ground in back of the mission in a haphazard manner, hoping to find the cache. Finally, the man watching the horses alerted them that travelers were arriving. The outlaws quickly mounted and disappeared.

On discovering the grizzly murder scene, angry citizens set out after the outlaws. A posse encountered the fleeing men south of San Luis Obispo. Two of them were killed in a gunfight and the remaining three were taken to Santa Barbara for trial. There they were tried and hung within the week.

It is believed that William Reed buried $200,000 in gold coins on the mission's grounds while he resided there. As far as is known, the treasure still lies there near where the victims of the massacre were found.

Chapter 8

El Muerto
The Headless Horseman

People living near the South Texas brush country known as the badlands, where the headless horseman began appearing around the year 1850, were not so much curious as they were terrified.

He was called El Muerto, the Dead One.
(Google Images.)

This ghostly rider seemed to appear everywhere, in cases causing panic, even more than that caused by the Indians, bandits and outlaws in the area.

This headless rider was called *El Muerto, the Dead One.* Attempts to explain him were fruitless, as were the efforts to destroy him.

The rider was always on the same dark horse. His head could not be seen under the large Mexican sombrero. He wore the light tan, rawhide leggings of the Mexican vaqueros, and a brush-torn serape that fluttered from his shoulders like a windblown cape.

Riflemen, who were excellent shots, claimed to have hit him, but they could never bring him down. Some accounts claimed that Indian arrows could be seen dangling from the body of the rider.

The origin of this Texas nightrider was kept secret for years. The headless horseman made his first appearance in Texas when the state was under siege from bandits and rustlers.

While the Texas Rangers did provide some protection for ranchers in the area, their numbers were small and the crimes were large.

It was at this time that Creed Taylor and "Big Foot" Wallace created their headless horror.

There was a huge chunk of land between the Rio Grande and the Nueces rivers that came to be known as "No Man's Land" and became a notorious hangout for outlaws.

Creed Taylor and his four brothers inherited a vast cattle empire from their father when he died in 1830. Taylor wasn't satisfied with this ranch, and decided to relocate on the eastern fringe of "No Man's Land."

He suffered miserable stock losses. Stock rustling was the primary sport for the Mexican *banditos* as well as the Comanche Indians. The Indians would eat their stolen goods.

The Mexican bandits, on the other hand, were more forward thinking. They simply altered the brands on the cattle they stole. When they had a herd large enough, they drove them to market, and sold them, usually at Brownsville or Matamoros.

In one year alone, more than 30,000 head of cattle disappeared from South Texas.

Creed Taylor decided he had had enough of these stock thieves. He knew that one well-known raider was a Mexican horse thief known as Vidal. After the Mexican made off with a string of his horses one early morning, Taylor and a neighbor, a Mexican cattleman named Flores, gave chase. A skilled tracker, Taylor and Flores followed Vidal and his gang to Uvalde, where they ran into Big Foot Wallace, a well-known frontiersman and an old friend of Taylor.

Big Foot was both eccentric and ingenious in his methods. He knew that Mexicans and Indians were extremely superstitious.

When the three found their quarry, Vidal and his men were sleeping. They were killed when they attempted to fight.

It was here that Big Foot's wily nature took over. Big Foot selected Vidal, who was wanted dead or alive by lawmen, to be the center of his plan. Vidal's head was severed from his body.

Then, Big Foot selected the wildest mustang in the stolen herd. This brute was incredibly strong and fast of foot. Its eyes blazed with fury and hate.

The three men lashed Vidal's body on the protesting horse. They bound his hands to the saddle horn, and tied his legs securely to the stirrups. Vidal's body was fashioned in the Mexican saddle so he couldn't possibly fall off.

When the body was lashed to the horse so that it couldn't flop nor fall, the terrified mustang was turned loose.

The scheme worked even better than Big Foot even dreamed.

His creation rode into Texas legend. Because the black horse never came near to anyone or anything, no one was able to kill it. It milled about on the fringes of vision, scaring everyone who saw it.

People credited the black horse and its headless rider with all kinds of curses and misfortune. Finally, a posse of local ranchers and cowboys were able to bushwhack the mustang at a watering hole.

They found the dried-up corpse of Vidal, his body riddle with hundreds of bullet holes, arrows and Indian spears. The body was lashed so securely to the horse and saddle that the rope had to be cut to loosen it.

What was left of Vidal was buried in a small cemetery on the La Trinidad ranch at Ben Bolt. El Muerto was now properly dead and buried.

Chapter 9

Arbuckles' Coffee

A cowboy just couldn't start his day without that wakeup with a strong cup of coffee. Whether at the ranch or on a cattle drive, that coffee was generally strong enough to float a horseshoe.

Until the end of the Civil War, coffee was sold green. It was up to the ranch cook or the chuck wagon cook to roast the beans on a wood stove or in a skillet over a campfire. This was no easy chore, for one burned bean ruined the whole batch.

Arbuckles' Coffee was the true cowboy's coffee.
(Google Images)

Ranch and trail cooks must have issued a sigh of relief when John Arbuckle announced in 1865 that he and his brother Charles were patenting a coffee roasting process that would eliminate the need for roasting.

61

Arbuckle coffee thus became a staple of the ranch and camp cook. Marketed under the name ARBUCKLES' ARIOSA COFFEE, in patented, airtight, one pound packages, the new coffee was an instant success with chuck wagon cooks in the west whose responsibility was keeping cowboys supplied with plenty of hot coffee out on the range.

The patented process included roasting and coating the coffee beans with an egg and sugar glaze to hold in the coffee flavor and aroma of the newly roasted beans. Arbuckle's coffee was distributed in the age before lined paper bags, and coffee went stale and rancid pronto.

Coating, or "glazing" as it came to be known, was a way to lengthen its shelf life by keeping air away from the beans. Many different compounds were used in the coffee trade. Arbuckle Bros. settled on a sugar-based glaze.

They became such a prodigious user of sugar that they decided to enter the sugar business rather than give a profit on the huge quantities they needed.

The Sugar Trust didn't like that much and decided to enter the coffee business to spite Arbuckle. For the better part of the next generation, the Sugar Trust's LION COFFEE battled it out with Arbuckle's brands throughout the courts and the cities of the nation. The first great advertising campaign in history was this coffee war.

After fighting to a standstill, the sugar boys quit the coffee business, and the Arbuckle brothers were triumphant. They strode upon the national stage until their deaths in the early part of the 20th Century.

ARBUCKLES' ARIOSA COFFEE packages bore a yellow label with the name ARBUCKLES' in large red letters across the front, beneath which flew a flying Angel trademark over the words ARIOSA COFFEE in black letters.

The coffee was shipped all over the country in sturdy wooden crates, one hundred packages to a crate. ARBUCKLES' ARIOSA COFFEE became so dominant, particularly in the west, that many Cowboys were not aware there was any other kind. With keen marketing minds, the Arbuckle Brothers printed signature coupons on the bags of coffee redeemable for all manner of notions including handkerchiefs, razors, scissors, and wedding rings.

To sweeten the deal, each package of ARBUCKLES' contained a stick of peppermint candy. This allowed the chuck wagon cook to offer an incentive to a cowboy to grind a fresh supply of coffee. The cowboy doing the grinding got the peppermint stick.

Upon hearing the cook's call, 'Who wants the candy?' some of the toughest cowboys on the trail were known to vie for the opportunity of manning the coffee grinder in exchange for satisfying a sweet tooth.

Arbuckle Bros. produced ARIOSA, known as "the coffee that won the West," and also roasted and packed several other popular brands, including their premium YUBAN brand, which was the best selling brand in New York for years.

Mr. John Arbuckle, who went on to become the greatest coffee roaster of his generation was also one of the richest men in America during the gilded age of the 1880s and '90s.

Improvement in Roasted Coffee.

To all whom it may concern:

"Be it known that I, John Arbuckle, Jr., of the city and county of Allegheny, in the State of Pennsylvania, have invented a new and useful Improvement in "Roasted Coffee;" and I do hereby declare that the following is a full and exact description thereof.

"The nature of my invention consists in roasting coffee and then coating it with a glutinous or gelatinous matter, for the purpose of retaining the aroma of the coffee, and also act as a clarifying-agent when the ground coffee has been boiled in water.

"To enable others skilled in the art of "roasting coffee" to use my invention, I will proceed to describe its operation or preparation.

"I take any good article of green coffee, and roast it by any of the known means. I then cool it as quickly as possible. I then prepare a mixture of the following ingredients, in about the following proportions: One ounce of Irish moss; half an ounce of isinglass; half an ounce of gelatine; one ounce of white sugar; and twenty-four eggs.

"I boil the Irish moss in a quart of water, and then strain it. I then boil the isinglass and gelatine in a pint of water. I then mix the sugar and eggs well together, and when the mixture of Irish moss, isinglass, gelatine, and water has become cold, I mix the whole of the ingredients into one homogenous compound.

"I then pour the whole over about one hundred pounds of the roasted coffee, and stir and so manipulate the coffee that each grain will be entirely coated, after the coffee is coated, and the coasting has become dry and hard, which is accomplished by forcing currents of air through it while stirring it, for the purpose of coating it with the glutinous or gelatinous matter described."

(Signed) John Arbuckle

Chapter 10

Legend of Blackbird Hill

The view from Blackbird Hill
to the Missouri River below.
(Google Images)

Eight miles north of Decatur, Nebraska, a hill stands on the Omaha Indian Reservation, overlooking the Missouri River. At its summit is a mound of dirt nearly 45 feet high. This mound marks the burial place of the great Omaha Indian Chief Blackbird.

Chief Blackbird was buried sitting upright on his favorite horse, which is the reason the mound is so high. Lewis and Clark visited the burial site in 1804, leaving behind decorations to commemorate the Chief.

Blackbird Hill is believed to be haunted. Each year, on October 17, people gather at the site. These people are not there anticipating the ghost of

Chief Blackbird, however, but that of a young woman who was murdered on the hill a century and a half ago.

The story concerns a young couple that had fallen in love in the 1840s. Descendants of Omaha Indians tell one version of the story. In this version, a band of Omaha Indians were hunting along the Missouri one afternoon when they came across a white man who was lost and starving.

His feet were bare and bleeding and what little remained of his clothing had been turned into rags. He was delirious and unable to speak. The Indians carried him back to their village and summoned their healer. The young man recovered, and during a brief stay while recuperating, told this story.

He and a young girl had fallen in love and planned to marry. But first, after finishing his schooling, the boy traveled abroad. He planned to return and marry his sweetheart. However, the boy never returned from his trip abroad.

While traveling abroad, the young man was involved in a shipwreck. He managed to survive this disaster, but it took him almost five years to work his way back to America. When he arrived home, he learned his mother had died, and worse, that his financè had married another man and moved west.

The devastated young girl waited for years for the boy's return, but finally gave him up for dead and married another man. The newlyweds headed west and settled on top of Blackbird Hill.

The girl's original fiancée, meanwhile, traveled all the way to California in search of his sweetheart. Unable to find her, he was returning home, traveling along the Missouri River.

While at the foot of Blackbird Hill, the young man saw a winding path leading up the slope and decided to follow it. It was on October 17, 1849, that the young girl saw her old fiancè walking up the winding path from the Missouri River. He was as surprised as she because he had no idea she lived there.

She confessed to him that she never stopped loving him, and that she had married her current husband only because she thought her first lover was dead.

The girl assured him that when her husband returned, she would tell him that she wished to be released from her marriage vows. They could then be together again and leave the next morning.

The young man hid in the woods while she informed her husband of her decision. Her husband did not take the news lightly and begged her to stay. When she refused, he attacked her with his hunting knife. She screamed and fell to the floor.

The husband dropped the knife and gathered up his bleeding wife. With her in his arms, he ran to the cliff and leaped, carrying her with him to the river far below.

The young man heard his former sweetheart's screams of agony, and ran after them, arriving just in time to see the husband leap over the cliff with his wife in his arms.

The young man collapsed with grief and wandered the hills until the band of Omaha Indians found him.

It is said that today, the path from the cabin to the edge of the cliff is barren. Even more than 150 years later, no plant life will grow there. It is also said that each year, on October 17, a woman's chilling scream can be herd at the top of the hill.

Blackbird Hill, itself, is located on the Omaha Indian Reservation, just west of Highway 75. It is eight miles north of Decatur along the Missouri River.

Chapter 11

The Buffalo Soldiers

More than 180,000 black Americans served in the Union Army during the civil war. Of these, more than 33,000 died.

After the Civil War, Congress was duly aware that the future of black Americans in the U.S. Army was in doubt. For this reason, Congress passed legislation establishing two cavalry and four infantry regiments, later consolidated into two, whose enlisted composition would be made up of black Americans.

The mounted regiments were the 9th and 10th Cavalries. The Plains Indians soon dubbed these units Buffalo Soldiers.

The military offered black Americans a rare opportunity for achievement in a bigoted society. The Buffalo Soldiers had the lowest desertion rate and the highest reenlistment rates in the frontier army.

The Buffalo Soldiers were set apart as paragons of military discipline. Racism, however, was still a big obstacle. This point was brought home when Henry O. Flipper, a quartermaster at a small Texas outpost, was discharged on trumped up charges in 1882.

Henry O. Flipper
(Google Images)

Flipper, who was born to a slave, was the first black American to graduate from West Point. He was unjustly discharged for embezzlement, but then went on to become a high-ranking official in the Interior Department. His name was cleared in 1976, years after his death.

The 9th and 10th Cavalries became well known for their service in subduing Mexican revolutionaries, hostile Native Americans, outlaws, comancheros, and rustlers.

Their services were accomplished over the most rugged and inhospitable territory in North America. Their adversaries included Geronimo, Sitting Bull, Victorio, Lone Wolf, Billy the Kid, and Pancho Villa.

Other services they performed, for which they were lesser known, was exploring and mapping vast areas of the southwest, where they helped string hundreds of miles of telegraph lines. They also built and repaired frontier outposts around which future towns and cities sprang to life.

In the late nineteenth and early twentieth centuries, the American Southwest was the scene of singular military experiments with firearms, clothing, transportation, and maneuvers.

In Arizona, white cavalrymen were assigned to study the use of camels for desert like warfare. It was a failure.

The 25th Infantry Bicycle Corps tests the bicycle at Fort Missoula, Montana, in Yellowstone National Park, 1896.
(Montana Historical Society)

An even more unique study by the army was the use of the nineteenth-century invention, the bicycle.

The black soldiers at Fort Huachuca in Arizona and soldiers in the Twenty-fifth Infantry, from Fort Missoula, Montana, tested bicycles as a means of military transportation.

For some unexplained reason, commanders in Washington, D.C. believed that black soldiers, although "good and true warriors", should be limited because of their "heritage and inclination" to assignments below the fortieth parallel.

The commanders believed that blacks could not tolerate cold northern temperatures.

The bicycle experiments were a failure for the army. The Buffalo Soldiers consistently received some of the worst assignments the army could offer. While performing these duties, they were scorned for their skin color and the color of their Union uniforms by citizens in the post-war frontier towns.

Buffalo Soldiers in the 9th Cavalry from a painting by L. Bjorkland. .   (Google Images)

Black American soldiers in Company B, 25th U.S. Infantry, stand at attention outside their barracks at Fort Randall, Dakota Territory.   (National Archives)

Recruitment of white officers to oversee the Buffalo Soldiers proved difficult. Both George Armstrong Custer and Frederick Benteen refused commissions with black American units.

The 9th Cavalry was ordered to Texas in June 1867. Among its charges was protecting stage and mail routes, building and maintaining forts, and establishing law and order.

Here is another Frederick Remington painting depicting black American soldiers. The men are in the Tenth Cavalry from Fort Huachuca, Arizona.
(American Heritage Center, University of Wyoming, Laramie)

The area was over-run with outlaws, Mexican revolutionaries and raiding Comanches, Cheyennes, Kiowas and Apaches. Many Texans saw the assignment of black troopers as a deliberate attempt by the Union to humiliate them.

Still, in the face of such prejudice, the 9th Cavalry established themselves as one of the most effective fighting forces in the Army.

During the 1860s and 70s, the frontier forts resembled little more than rundown villages. The enlisted men's barracks lacked good ventilation and were little more than vermin infested hovels. Bathing facilities consisted of the local creek.

As a result, the black soldiers suffered diseases such as dysentery, diarrhea, bronchitis and tuberculosis. Rations were most often beef or bacon, beans, fresh vegetables from the post garden, and sometimes fruit or jam.

The workweek was seven days, except for the fourth of July and Christmas. The monthly pay for a private was thirteen dollars.

In their off hours, many of the black soldiers availed themselves of education classes. Chaplains assigned to the black units taught the classes as part of a program to alleviate illiteracy mandated by slavery.

While desertion was the most serious problem faced by the Army during the Indian War period, desertion was about twenty-five percent higher in white units than among the Black units.

For more than twenty years the 9th and 10th Cavalry Regiments served on the frontier from Montana to Texas, along the Rio Grande in New Mexico, Arizona, Colorado and the Dakotas. The conditions the Buffalo Soldiers fought in, while pursuing the Apache, are described in a letter from Colonel Hatch to General Pope:

"...the work performed by these troops is most arduous, horses worn to mere shadows, men nearly without boots, shoes and clothing. That the loss in horses may be understood when following the Indians in the Black Range the horses were without anything to eat five days except what they nibbled from piñon pines, going without food so long was nearly as disastrous as the fearful march into Mexico of 79 hours without water, all this by forced marches over inexpressibly rough trails...It is impossible to describe the exceeding roughness of such mountains as the Black Range and the San Mateo. The well known Modoc Lava beds are a lawn compared with them." (Hatch to Pope, February 25, 1880)

While the Buffalo Soldiers had no role in the slaughter of 146 men, women and children in The Battle at Wounded Knee on December 29, 1891, it was their last campaign on the frontier.

Chapter 12

Tilting at Windmills

Windmills built in North America were different in design and appearance from those used in England and on the continent of Europe. European windmills served valuable roles, such as grinding grain in gristmills, but they were expensive to build and needed constant human attention.

Windmills were the dominant means of bring water to arid prairie farm such as this one in Wyoming.
(Wyoming State Museum)

According to the *Windmillers Gazette,* Daniel Halladay designed the first commercially successful windmill in the New World

Halladay's windmill had a self-governing design. It would automatically face the wind even though the wind might shift directions. It also controlled its own speed of operation.

The inventor built his first successful self-governing windmill in Connecticut and the company manufactured from there from 1854 to 1863. Because there were delays in production and shipping, caused partly by the American Civil War, Halladay moved his factory to Batavia, Illinois.

There, in the Fox River Valley, Halladay Standard windmills sold by the thousands to farmers and ranchers across the prairies of North America.

Halladay received a challenge to his windmill design in 1867 when the Reverend Leonard H. Wheeler invented the Eclipse model windmills.

Wheeler and his son devised their windmill for use at their mission. Instead of having a wheel composed of pivoting sections, their wind machine had a solid wheel where components were rigidly fastened together.

In addition, the Wheelers attached their wheel to a hinged vane, or tail, which operated like a weather vane, keeping the wheel pointed toward the wind.

During early windmill production, all windmills in North America were built of wood. All-metal windmills were introduced in the 1870s.

The use of metal allowed windmill manufacturers to create wind wheels containing curved blades, making them more efficient than wooden blades.

Chapter 13

Quanah Parker
Last Comanche Chief

Quanah Parker, the last Chief of the Comanches, never lost a battle to the white man.

He was the son of an Indian Chief, Peta Nocona, who himself had been chief of the Quahada Comanche.

Quanah refused to accept the provisions of the *1867 Treaty of Medicine Lodge.* The terms of the treaty would confine the Southern Plains Indians to a reservation. He was also suspect of the provisions that promised to clothe the Indians and turn them into farmers like the white settlers.

Quanah Parker
(Texas Collections,
Baylor University)

The young chief opted to remain on the warpath, raiding in Texas and Mexico and out-maneuvering Army Colonel Ronald S. Mackenzie.

The standoff against the U.S. Government reached a point where Quanah's allies were weary and starving. Colonel Mackenzie sent Jacob J. Sturm, a physician and post interpreter, to solicit Quanah's surrender.

Sturm pleaded his case with Quanah, who then rode to a mesa. There, from the top of the mesa, he saw a wolf come toward him, howl and trot away. Overhead, he watched an eagle glide lazily, and then flap it wings in the direction of Fort Sill.

These were signs, Quanah thought, and he and his band surrendered at Fort Sill, Oklahoma.

While Quanah decided to travel the white man's road, he did it in his own way. He refused, for example, to give up polygamy, something that was very disturbing to the reservation agent. The reservation agent, an appointee of the Federal Government, felt his duty was to destroy all vestiges of Native American life and replace it with the white man's.

Quanah was a true leader. He negotiated grazing rights with Texas cattlemen, invested in a railroad, and even more disturbing to the reservation agent, he used peyote.

He learned the English language and became a reservation judge. Quanah lobbied Congress and pleaded the cause of the Comanche Nation. He counted among his friends cattleman Charles Goodnight (who established the Goodnight Trail) and President Theodore Roosevelt.

Cynthia Ann Parker

Quanah's mother, Cynthia Ann Parker, was a white girl abducted by the Comanches at the age of 9. Taken with her were her brother, John, 6, Elizabeth Kellogg, Rachel Plummer, with child, and her son James.

Cynthia Ann Parker
(Google Images)

Elizabeth and Rachel were in their teens and sold to other tribes as slaves. General Sam Houston paid a ransom of $150 for Elizabeth. Two years later, Rachel was found half-crazed from the loss of her little boy James. She witnessed also the killing of her newborn baby by the Indians (because it cried too much).

Cynthia Ann was taken to live with a band of Comanches called People. She was given to a Tenowish Comanche couple that dressed her after the Indian fashion, fed and cared for her as their own child.

The Comanches named her *Naduah,* meaning "keeps warm with us." She learned the Indian ways as the years wore on and her own blood kin faded.

One day, a white trader from the east stared at the blue eyes of Naduah and asked to trade for her. A young brave, Peta Nocona, told the trader that he would never trade anything for her, as she did not want to leave. Moreover, she loved Peta Nocona and he loved her.

Peta became a War Chief. His new band of Comanche warriors was called Nawkonnee (Wanderers). Following one big raid, Peta came home driving a string of horses to Naduah's tent. He wanted her for his wife.

Naduah bore three children for Peta Nocona, the eldest being Quanah. It is noted that Peta never took other wives, as was the Comanche custom, indicating his love of Naduah.

Some accounts claim that her brother John Parker, who had been captured along with her, tried in the mid-1840s to persuade her to return to her white family. She refused, explaining that she loved her husband and children too much to leave them.

Eventually, after fearing her husband and sons had been killed during a raid, Naduah was persuaded to return to the home of her uncle Isaac Parker. She made several attempts to return to her Indian people, but was thwarted in each attempt.

In 1910, her son, Quanah moved her body to Post Oak Cemetery near Cache, Oklahoma. She was later moved to Fort Sill, Oklahoma, and re-interred beside Quanah.

Comanche

Comanche, a survivor.
(Google Images)

For at least a generation, Comanche was the most famous horse in America. Comanche was the only living thing the U.S. Cavalry got back from the Battle of Little Big Horn.

When reinforcements arrived, Custer and all his soldiers were dead. The Indians took all of the surviving horses with the exception of Comanche that was injured.

The horse was nursed back to health and became a living symbol of Manifest Destiny. The public loved him, thinking he was Custer's horse (he wasn't).

This was fine with the Army. They wanted the public on their side while they killed Indians. Comanche toured the country and became a favorite in parades and patriotic gatherings.

Chapter 14

The Automobile Fad

Charles and Frank Duryea are credited with
building the first American car.

(Google Images)

Gasoline in 1902 was sixty cents per gallon. It
was difficult to get. If there was no drug store
handy where it could be purchased, it could be
found at a hardware or paint store.

However, hardware and paint stores might sell
customers benzene for gasoline. For the car owner,
it was custom to carry two five-gallon cans of gas
and a gallon of oil in reserve.

America's first gasoline powered commercial car
manufacturers were two brothers, Charles and
Frank Duryea. The brothers first made bicycles

before becoming interested in gasoline engines and automobiles.

The brothers tested their first automobile, the one-cylinder "Buggyaut" on the streets of Springfield, Massachusetts on September 21, 1893. It is considered the first successful gas-engine vehicle built in the U.S.

In 1895, a second Duryea, driven by J. Frank Duryea, won the *Chicago Times-Herald* race in Chicago on a snowy Thanksgiving Day. He traveled 54 miles at an average of 7.5 miles per hour, marking the first US auto race in which any entrants finished.

Charles Duryea founded the Duryea Motor Wagon Company in 1896. It was the first company to manufacture and sell gasoline-powered vehicles. The company sold 13 cars by the end of 1896.

The brothers went their separate ways by the end of the century. J. Frank helped produce the Stevens-Duryea while Charles produced Duryea vehicles as late as 1917.

Two months after the Duryea Brothers sold their first commercial vehicle, New York City motorist Henry Wells hit a bicyclist with his new Duryea. This was the first recorded automobile accident. The bicyclist suffered a broken leg and Wells spent the night in jail.

Henry Ford entered the car scene in 1903, proclaiming, "I will build a car for the great multitude." He followed through on this promise, offering, in October 1908, the Model "T" for $950.

Ford's 1932 model had the Ford V8 Engine.
(Google Images)

The 1949 Ford took another distinctive style turn.
(Google Images)

1965 Mustang was one of Ford's most enduring models.
(Google Images)

The Model "T" heralded the beginning of the motor age. During its nineteen years of production, the price for the Model "T" dropped as low as $280. Nearly 15,500,000 Model Ts were sold in the United States alone.

Legend says that Henry Ford told his designers, "You can paint it any color you want as long as it's black." While historians haven't proved this remark, black was obviously Ford's choice.

Ford revolutionized manufacturing. By the year 1914, his Highland Park, Michigan plant could turn out a complete chassis every 93 minutes. His mass production techniques eventually speeded the manufacture of a Model "T" to even faster rates.

The automobile baron moved ahead of car companies with wages paid. In 1914, he began paying his employees five dollars a day, near double what other companies paid.

In 1932, Henry Ford introduced his last great personal engineering triumph, the "en block" or one piece, V-8 engine. The engine enabled the 1932 Ford to outperform all other popular car models. It was considered to be 20-years ahead of its time.

It was Edsel Ford, Henry Ford's only son, that steered the Ford Motor Company into classier and sleeker looking automobiles.

Edsel became secretary of Ford Motor Company in 1915, and in 1919, assumed the firm's presidency. He advocated the introduction of a more modern automobile to replace the Model "T". He was repeatedly over-ruled by his father.

When Model "T" sales began to plummet, the elder Ford allowed the company to begin working on the Model "A".

Henry Ford oversaw the mechanical quality and reliability of the Model A, but left it to Edsel to flesh out the body design. Edsel collaborated with designer Jozsef Galamb in designing the car.

Even though Edsel was often at loggerheads with his father on major decisions, he was able to accomplish several lasting changes. For instance, he founded the Mercury division, which strengthened Ford's overseas production. Edsel was responsible, too, for the Lincoln Zephyr and the Lincoln Continental.

He died in 1943, at age 49 of cancer. His father Henry then resumed the presidency of Ford.

Chapter 15

The Greatest Land Buy!

With one stroke of the pen, the United States doubled its size. The deal was the magnificent Louisiana Purchase, which opened a large tract of land to settlement, and assured the free navigation of the Mississippi.

Thomas Jefferson, in a single action, doubled the size of the U.S.
(Kirby Collection, Lafayette College.)

It might have been the biggest coup for any U.S. president, and it happened almost as a stroke of luck.

The United States was too interested in settling the land east of the Mississippi to take much interest in the West, with the exception of the fur trade.

In 1800, however, an event happened that changed matters. France extracted control from Spain of the immense territory called Louisiana. This included the port in New Orleans, at its southern extremity.

New Orleans was the gateway to the world for the whole of the Mississippi Basin and all the American agricultural products that moved down the river.

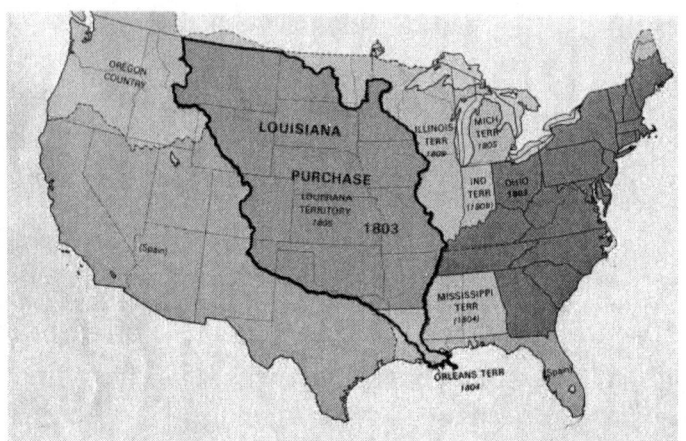

Jefferson's aquizition of the Louisiana Purchase doubled the size of the United States. (Google Images)

President Thomas Jefferson feared that Napoleon might be bold enough to interfere with U.S. trade through New Orleans. Jefferson decided to try and buy the city of New Orleans from the French.

To Jefferson's surprise, Napoleon, who was strapped for cash, made a counter-offer that amounted to what may be the greatest real estate bargain in history. He offered to sell the entire Louisiana Territory for about $15 million

It is true, the land was an unmapped wilderness, but it included 800,000 square miles of land stretching from the Mississippi River to the Rocky Mountains, from the Gulf Coast to the Canadian Border.

Jefferson, by signing the treaty, doubled the geographical area of the United States.

Even so, there were many critics who claimed that the U.S. had its hands full trying to settle the still-wild states and territories, including Kentucky, Tennessee, and Mississippi.

Jefferson dispatched two able Army officers, Meriwether Lewis and William Clark, on an expedition to explore the unknown realm of the newly acquired territory.

Lewis and Clark left St. Louis on May 14, 1804. In their party were 28 soldiers, a half-Indian interpreter, and a black slave named York. They set off on the Missouri River in three boats and by fall, had reached what is now North Dakota. Here, they wintered with the friendly Mandan Indians.

It was here, too, that the Lewis and Clark party took on another valuable addition to the party. This was a 16-year-old Indian woman named Sacajawea, the pregnant wife of a French-Canadian trapper who also joined the expedition.

Sacajawea gave birth before the group set off in the spring. She carried her infant son while trudging up rugged mountain trails, and even while thrashing down whitewater streams in a canoe.

It was Sacajawea that guided Lewis and Clark over the Rockies and along the Columbia River to the Pacific. She did many things. She interpreted for them, she rescued their gear when a boat capsized, and she obtained horses from local Indians.

Even though Sacajawea showed the explorers the way west, in the journals of Lewis and Clark she was merely recorded as "the Indian woman," because they could not spell her name.

Sacajawea was an Indian guide for Lewis and Clerk when they made their historic trek west. Here she signals to a party of Chinook Indians in a painting by Charles M. Russell. (Amon Carter Museum, Fort Worth, Texas)

Lewis and Clark returned east two years and ten days from the time they departed to go west on an exploration trip. Their topographic sketches showed people how they could reach the Pacific Ocean.

Their reports on the rich beaver supply in western rivers set off a rush by trappers, such as Jim Bridger, Jedediah Smith, and the Sublette brothers, William and Milton.

Even though Jefferson pushed both his Louisiana Purchase and the funding to map the territory through congress, he never did see it. Jefferson never traveled further west than Harper's Ferry, West Virginia.

Chapter 16

The Rape of Monterey

David Jack immigrated to California at 26-years-of-age, bent on making a fortune. Gold had just been found and he knew fortunes could be made there, if not in gold, then in other ways.

David Jacks, Monterey County, California land baron. (Google Images)

Jack took his total savings of $1400 and invested it in revolvers. These he intended to sell at a handsome profit when he arrived in California.

His vision was correct. On arrival in San Francisco, Jack sold the entire lot in less than 48 hours for $4,000, making a profit of 286 percent.

He then ventured to the gold mines, found little success, and didn't linger long. He returned to San Francisco where he took a job as an inspector in the Custom House, earning $100 a month.

Always on the lookout for moneymaking opportunities, he put his $4,000 capital from the sale of the revolvers to work, loaning the money out at an interest rate of two per cent per month.

During a trip to Monterey in 1850, David Jack recognized the vast potential of the area. Monterey, at that time, was a town with less than 1,000 people. Jack moved there the next year.

He worked as a clerk in Joseph Boston's general store on Olivier Street and boarded with Boston and his family at their palatial home on Van Buren Street. Jack vowed that one day he would own the property. Later on in his life, he did buy it.

Jack then worked as a clerk for James McKinley, a Scottish pioneer who owned a dry goods store in Monterey. At the same time, Jack became involved in the growing of potatoes, a crop he believed would be successful in California's bustling mining communities.

He fell victim to both a falling market and to schemers and speculators. He was forced to sell hogs he had purchased at $3,000 for $50. But these economic disasters did not deter the young Scotsman.

In 1830, the Mexican government granted 30,000 acres of land to the City of Monterey. When California became a state, the new governor faced the problem of settling land claims of the former Mexican province. Under Mexican law, there were three main dispositions of land.

First, there were the large "ranchos", which included extensive land grants to the early Spanish settlers and their descendants. Second, there were the mission properties, including the church, its gardens and outbuildings and additional acreage held in trust for the Indian neophytes. And third, there were the pueblo lands that were allotted for use of the community and its citizens.

David Jack purchase property in 1853 that included

the present site of Pebble Beach golf course and other exclusive areas. (Google Images)

In 1853, Jack's big opportunity surfaced. The City of Monterey hired attorney Delos Rodeyn Ashley to legitimize its claims to 29,698.53 acres of land before the United States Land Claims Commission in San Francisco. Ashley was successful and presented the City of Monterey with a legal bill of $991.50.

The town's coffers were bare, and even the paltry legal bill was beyond the city's ability to pay.

The State Legislature therefore passed a bill, which allowed Monterey to auction off its town lands to pay the debt.

On February 9, 1859, on the steps of Colton Hall, all 29,698.53 acres of Monterey pueblo lands were auctioned off. The sole bidders were David Jack and Delos Ashley. The selling price was $1,002.50, all of which was given to Ashley. The lawyer sold his interest to Jack a number of years later.

Jack thus became the owner of 30,000 acres of magnificent, scenic countryside surrounding Monterey as well as the town itself. The City of Monterey tried twice, unsuccessfully, to reclaim the lost lands. The case went all the way to the U.S. Supreme Court, which ruled in Jack's favor.

Jack soon learned that the *Californios* that had been granted lands in the Salinas area were more adept in their saddles than they were in tending to business. Many of these *rancheros* became pressed for money during the dry years. They were forced to sell cattle at ridiculous prices and became lax in their payment of taxes.

The enterprising David Jack began paying these overdue taxes on the best land. Eventually, Jack foreclosed on defaulted mortgages, and, piece-by-piece, added to his holdings. At one time, it was estimated that Jack owned 100,000 acres of Monterey County lands.

He didn't accumulate his holdings without incurring the wrath of the native peoples of Monterey County. Those that lost their lands to

Jack considered him a land thief, while Jack considered them to be "squatters" on his property.

One group formed what they called "The Squatters League of Monterey County". In 1872 the League wrote to Jack:

You have been the cause of unnecessary annoyance and expense to the settlers (and) now if you don't make that account of damages to each and every one of us within ten days, you son of a bitch, we will suspend your animation between daylight and hell.

Jack amassed large land holdings in Monterey. The pueblo lands alone were the richest and most valuable property in California, consisting, as they did, of the present-day cities of Pacific Grove, Del Rey Oaks, Seaside, the Del Monte Forest, Fort Ord, and the spectacular Seventeen-Mile-Drive.

The resourceful Scotsman developed interests in the dairy business. He soon owned partnerships in 14 dairies in the Salinas Valley. When faced with an oversupply of milk, the dairies produced their own cheese that had origins traced to the Spanish Franciscan fathers that had come to California from Mexico in the early days of the missions.

The cheese was marketed as "Jacks Cheese", and it became very popular on the west coast. People began asking for it by name and "Monterey Jack" became synonymous with this white creamy cheese.

While many credited Jack with the development and marketing of this cheese, there were a number of other persons that manufactured similar cheese before David Jack. One such person was Domingo Pedrazzi of Carmel Valley, California. Pedrazzi used a "house jack" to apply pressure during the cheese-making process, hence the names "jack" cheese.

Some of the controversy may have been due to the fact that David Jack was known in California as David Jacks. When or why the "s" was added to his surname is a matter of conjecture.

Kenneth Jack, who wrote an account on his famous and distant relative, believes the "s" was added through common usage. Jack owned so much land and property, and with Jacks being a more possessive sounding name, people would refer to property or places owned by him, such as "David Jack's Church," "Jack's Peak," "Jack's Cheese," etc. It is thought that Jack himself perhaps liked the name in its plural form.

Chapter 17

Zebulon Montgomery Pike
He Never Climbed the Peak

Zebulon M. Pike was a poor explorer with a knack for getting lost. He began his exploration activities in 1805, when he left St. Louis with 20 men and a keelboat full of supplies to locate the source of the Mississippi River.

Zebulon M. Pike
(Google Images)

History notes the effort was both poorly planned and ill timed. He left half his men behind when he reached Little Falls, in what is now Minnesota.

He pressed forward by sled to Leech Lake, which he proudly but erroneously identified as the Mississippi's source.

Pike just couldn't get anything right. He hardly finished his report on the source of the Mississippi when he received another assignment. He was ordered to seek out the headwaters of the Arkansas and Red rivers to the southwest.

Pike's Peak   (Google Images)

The orders came from James Wilkinson, governor of Louisiana Territory. Wilkinson was suspected of receiving money from the Spanish Crown in return for information on American military movements. Whether Pike was an unwitting tool or co-conspirator to Wilkinson remains a mystery.

On this new voyage to find the source of the Arkansas and Red rivers, Pike took with him 18 enlisted men who had accompanied him on his search for Mississippi's source.

He described his crew as "a Dam'd set of Rascels (sic)." In addition to the enlisted men, Governor Wilkinson's son, a lieutenant in the army, an interpreter, and a civilian doctor named John Hamilton Brown, were part of Pike's party. Pike went up the Missouri and Osage rivers to the Republican, then south to the Arkansas, which he followed to the Front Range of the Rockies. He wintered at the present site of Pueblo, Colorado.

In the spring, Pike took his group over the Sangre de Cristo Mountains and eventually emerged on the upper Rio Grande. Here, Spanish troops arrested Pike for spying. They confiscated his maps and notes and escorted him across northern Mexico to Nacogdoches, and dumped him on the American side of the border.

He is best remembered for making claims that the plains region he crossed was a great American desert and was fundamentally uninhabitable. Future settlement proved him wrong. Nevertheless, his foreboding picture kept settlers from venturing west for years.

As Pike crossed his "sandy deserts" he noticed a distant mountain, which appeared much like a "small blue cloud" to him. When his party crested a hill, laid out before the explorers were the grand panorama of the southern Rockies.

The sight inspired Pike's men to give "three cheers to the Mexican mountains". Pike decided to climb the peak that had so caught his attention before. As he was prone to do, he badly misjudged the mountain's ruggedness.

He found distances in the clear, dry air of what is now Colorado were deceptive. Thinking the hike would only take a few hours, Pike and three men, clad in light cotton overalls and no stockings, set out to climb the peak.

On the morning of the fourth day, following a camp without food, water, or blankets, the group reached a minor summit. They discovered, however, that the mountain's real summit was still miles away and as high again as the one they had just climbed.

It appeared barren and icy. Pike concluded that no human being could climb it to its pinnacle.

Historians note that this was as close as Pike came to the peak that bears his name.

Pike's expedition didn't improve. When he passed Royal Gorge on the Arkansas River, he turned north in search of the Spanish patrol. He found instead, another substantial river he believed to be the Red.

He believed he was now heading home and followed the stream downward. Four weeks later, he found himself back at Royal Gorge. His Red River had actually been the Arkansas.

He wrote, ...*this was my 28th birthday, and most fervently did I hope never to pass another so miserably.*

Troubles for the young explorer didn't end there. He and his men attempted to cross the Sangre de Cristo Mountains (In what is now New Mexico) in the middle of winter. The men went for days without food and many nights without sleep. Nine of his 13 men developed frozen feet.

Pike was forced to make the heart-rending decision to leave those behind who could no longer travel with the party. After two weeks, he found a pass that brought him into the San Luis Valley.

On a stream he believed was the Red River, he built a fort and sent five volunteers back to rescue the men left behind. All were saved.

To his consternation, Pike learned it wasn't the Red River he was camped by at all. It was the Rio Grande. He and his men were escorted to Santa Fe, where his notes and papers were confiscated. The party was then moved to Chihuahua, and finally, by a long, circuitous route, back across Texas to the American border post at Natchitoches on the Red River.

This was the very spot Pike was supposed to have reached a year earlier from a different direction.

Chapter 18

Sam Brannan

Sam Brannan is the man that touched off the powder keg of "gold mania" that brought the world to California and other parts of the west. Brannan came west leading a party of 200 gold-hungry people from New York.

Brannan's arrival with the 200 potential gold miners immediately tripled the population of Yerba Buena (now called San Francisco).

Sam Brannan
(California State Library)

By the time James Marshall discovered gold at Sutter's Mill, Brannan already owned a newspaper, a hotel, a flour mill, and a store. He opened several more general stores, one of which was a store at Sutter's Fort. It was indeed part of Brannan's scheme, since he would profit by selling goods to the miners.

John Sutter and James Marshall wanted to keep the gold discovery a secret. Sutter wanted to finish construction of his sawmill first.

Sam Brannan's store at Sutter's Fort.
(Google Images)

Sutter offered his workmen double wages if they would keep the gold discovery a secret. He asked them to continue working on the sawmill during the week and look for gold on Sundays.

Brannan, editor of the California Star, a one-page San Francisco newspaper, had other plans after he heard of the gold discovery.

He was still in his 20s and soon was California's first millionaire. He shamelessly used the tithes of the Mormon Church for personal profit by investing in real estate and other ventures.

Brigham Young, head of the Mormon Church, dispatched an agent from Salt Lake City to recover "the Lord's money."

Brannan's reply to the messenger, "You go back and tell Brigham that I'll give up the Lord's money when he sends me a receipt signed by the Lord."

Soon after, Brannan was officially "disfellowshipped" from the church. He ignored the order of excommunication and continued to collect tithes to the church.

For several weeks after he learned of Marshall's discovery, Brannan bought everything in the region that might be useful to gold miners. He stored the goods in a warehouse near his store at Sutter's Fort.

Then, on May 12, 1848, Brannan appeared in the plaza at San Francisco waving a bottle of gold dust and began shouting, "Gold! Gold! Gold from the American River."

People rushed to get gold mining supplies.

When the rumors reached Monterey, they were not believed. On June 6, Walter Colton, *alcalde* or mayor of Monterey, sent a messenger to the American River to verify the gold discovery.

When the messenger came back with samples of gold, Colton said, "The blacksmith dropped his hammer, the carpenter his plane, the mason his trowel, the farmer his sickle, and they were all off to the mines.

Some went with horses, some on carts and some on crutches, and one even went on a litter.

"These gold mines," Colton moaned, are going to upset all the domestic arrangements of society."

Colonel Richard B. Mason could not prevent his soldiers from deserting, especially after one of them returned from a three-week furlough with a quantity of gold worth more than his army salary for five years.

It was a crazy scene in California. By the end of 1848 about four thousand men from various parts of California and about six thousand more from places like Hawaii, Oregon, Utah, Mexico, Peru and Chili were all at the California diggings.

Sam Brannan was taking in $150,000-a-month selling gold mining equipment and other supplies to the gold seekers. He no longer had need for the tithes he had been collecting.

Vicente Perez Rosales, a Chilean gold miner, described Brannan's store at Sutter's Fort. "We saw there a cabin of unfinished boards, a few huts of woven branches and a short distance away a large store with a huge sign that read, 'Brannan and Company'."

By 1856, Brannan was said to have owned one fifth of the entire city of San Francisco and as much of Sacramento. He was said to be earning as much as $250,000 to $500,000 per year.

An affinity for whiskey and a bitter divorce settlement finally led to his financial ruin.

Chapter 19

Will James
His Books and His Art

(Author's Note: Nobody grew up reading more of Will James' material than did the author. His stories were the very embodiment of what many kids wanted to be, a cowboy. Will James made it happen for them, if only in their imagination, even though many never went near a horse.)

W ill James summed up his life's dream in the preface of his first book. He wrote:

I am a cowboy, and what's put down in these pages is not material that I've hunted up, it's what I've lived, seen, and went thru before I ever had any ideas that my writing and sketches would ever appear before the public.

The story of Will James is almost a lonely one and his writing often depicted that loneliness.

Will was born Joseph-Ernest Dufault in Quebec, Canada on June 6, 1892. He hated the name so much that he changed it to William Roderick James about 1910.

During his early years, James worked as a bronc buster and as a cowboy on various ranches in Montana, Idaho and Nevada. In 1914, he was arrested for cattle rustling, and served a little over a year in Nevada State Prison at Carson City.

Will James self-portrait.
(Google Images)

He was 22-years-old at the time and was denied parole at least twice before being released in April 1916. This may have been the turning point in his life as far as his art was concerned.

To pass the long hours in prison, James began making drawings. He decided that this might be the career he wanted to follow. In his parole application, James wrote:

I have a natural talent for drawing and during my imprisonment have done considerable of this work. It is my ambition to go east and study art and I feel that if given an opportunity to develop this talent my future will be assured. As a sample for your inspection I am submitting a few samples drawn by myself.

In 1919, while riding a bucking bronco, James was bucked off, and fell head first into a railroad track. This incident left him with a severe

concussion and pretty much ended his life as a
rodeo   cowboy.

Western artist Will James was noted
for his accuracy in drawing an
animal's correct conformation.
(University of Nevada, Reno)

James seems to be doing self-
portraits when he paints his
horses and cowboys.

While recuperating in a Reno hospital, a fellow patient recognized James' talent for drawing and gave him a letter of introduction to Sunset Magazine. James sold a series of drawings to Sunset, the first of which was published in 1920.

Also in 1920, James married Alice Conradt, of Reno. He continued working as an illustrator, but also earned income as a ranch hand. They lived in various places, including Nevada, Arizona and New Mexico, and finally in Montana.

Alice encouraged him to develop his natural story-telling ability. In one week, James wrote and illustrated an article entitled, "Bucking Horses and Bucking-Horse Riders."

He submitted the article and twelve drawings to *Scribners*, a leading New York magazine. Scribners published the article in 1923, and it was so well received the magazine asked James to become a regular contributor.

He wrote and illustrated six more stories for the magazine over the next twelve months. These seven stories, along with another published in the *Saturday Evening Post* comprised James first book, "Cowboys North and South", published by Scribners in 1924. In 1925, Scribners published a second book, "The Drifting Cowboy".

All of his writing and artwork was based on his actual experience as a cowboy. His language was colorful, but as an illustrator of horseflesh, James was considered second-to-none.

In 1926, Will James put a down payment on several thousand acres in the Pryor Mountains of Montana, 45 miles south of Billings. He and Alice moved there the next year and took up cattle ranching.

In 1934, Will returned to Canada one last time and attempted to burn everything that linked him to Ernest Dufault. He didn't want the public, his publisher, his wife or friends to know that he was really Ernest Dufault from Quebec.

James kept the secret of his real name to himself. Not even his wife was aware of it until a dispute arose over the estate. The dispute forced James brother, Auguste, to prove that Ernest Dufault and Will James were the same person.

His wife, Alice, left James in 1935 after fifteen years. His excess drinking ruined both his marriage and his health.

James left his Rocking R ranch and moved into a cellar with the Snook family. He later moved to Hollywood, California, where he died from alcoholic complications September 3, 1942.

The ranch where Will and Alice lived in Montana is now a featured stop on the self-guided driving tour of the Frenchman River Valley.

Chapter 20

'Sequoyah' developed
The Cherokee Alphabet

At a dinner party in England, William Waldorf Astor made a bet. Astor wagered that he could produce a cross-section of a redwood tree that would be large enough to form a table for forty guests.

Sequoyah, who developed the Cherokee Indian alphabet. (Google Images)

He proved good on his wager by shipping a redwood cross section that measured two-feet thick. The diameter varied from 16 feet six inches at one point to fourteen feet eleven inches at another.

This meant the giant slab had a circumference of some fifty-two feet, which is large enough to seat forty men rather comfortably. Given the slab's substantial measurements, its size is still considered small. Many redwoods in California reach a circumference of sixty feet, and some have been reported as large as seventy-five feet.

Sequoia redwood trees are named in honor of Sequoyah, the Cherokee Indian who invented letters for his people.

It is likely that Sequoyah was born handicapped, as the Cherokee word for Sikwo-yl means *pig's foot.*

Sequoyah fled Tennessee as a youth because of encroachment from white settlers. He initially moved to Georgia, where he acquired skill in working with silver.

Sequoia redwoods are the largest trees in existence. (Google Images)

While there, a man who purchased one of his works suggested that he sign the piece as the white silversmiths do.

Sequoyah did not know how to write, so he visited Charles Hicks, a wealthy farmer who wrote English.

Hicks showed Sequoyah how to write his name, writing the letters on a piece of paper. Sequoyah began to toy with the idea of a Cherokee writing system. The year was 1809.

Later, Sequoyah moved to Willstown, Alabama, and enlisted in the Cherokee Regiment. He fought in the Battle of Horseshoe Bend, which ended the war against the Creek Redsticks. During the war, Sequoyah became convinced of the necessity of literacy for his people. He and other Cherokees were unable to write letters home, read military orders, or record events as they happened.

He began in earnest to create a writing system. He used a phonetic system, where each sound in speech was represented by a symbol.

His alphabet was listed as officially complete in 1821. It took Sequoyah twelve years to create the Cherokee alphabet.

When Sequoyah started, he tried using pictographs. He soon discovered that the number of symbols in the Cherokee language would be in the thousands.

He decided instead to create symbols for each syllable used by the Cherokee. Sequoyah did not receive the support of Cherokee leaders at first. They considered the written language as "the work of the devil".

Sequoyah created the "Talking Leaves", 85 letters that make up the Cherokee syllabary. He would later add another symbol, making the total 86.

His daughter, Ayoka, easily learned the method of communication. Sequoyah demonstrated the syllabary to his cousin, George Lowrey, by sending Ayoka outside the house, then asking Lowrey to answer a question.

Sequoyah wrote the answer on a piece of paper. He then had Ayoka read the answer aloud to

Lowrey, who then urged Sequoyah to demonstrate the syllabary in public.

Later, in a Cherokee court in Chattooga, Sequoyah read an argument about a boundary line from a sheet of paper. Word spread quickly of the young Cherokee's invention. Twelve years after the original idea, the Cherokee Nation adopted Sequoyah's alphabet.

As a consequence, within months thousands of Cherokee became literate.

Sequoyah then moved west to Arkansas. He mined and sold salt to earn money, and became active in politics.

In 1824, the National council at New Echota struck a silver medal in Sequoyah's honor. Later, publication began on the first Native American newspaper., *The Cherokee Phoenix* in the same town.

Chapter 21

The Farallones
'Islands of the Dead'

First discovered by Native Americans, the Farallones were called "Islands of the Dead". The Indians refused to set foot on them for spiritual reasons.

A lighthouse stands guard on the Farallones.
(Harper's New Monthly Magazine)

The first known person to set foot on the Farallones was Sir Francis Drake who made a stop there on one of his journeys westward.

Drake called the outcroppings the "Islands of St. James," but in 1769, another explorer, Juan

Francisco de Bodega, renamed them *Los Farallones de los Frailes.*

The tiny islands remained unaffected by human interference until 1810, when New England sealing boats spent two years at the Farallones slaughtering more than 150,000 Northern Fur Seals.

Following the New Englanders came Russian Fur Traders, who set up camp at Fort Ross, and spent several years further massacring the Northern Fur Seal. When there were few seals left, and their hunting was no longer profitable, the Russians left in 1841.

Farallon is a Spanish word meaning a small pointed islet in the sea.

These rocks are probably of volcanic origin, bare and desolate, and lie in a line curiously like the islands of Hawaii. Some geologists claim they are the outcrops of an immense granite dike.

The southernmost and largest of the Farallones is also the largest, as is the island of Hawaii in the Hawaiian Islands. The largest Farallon island extends about 340 feet high.

Teddy Roosevelt declared the North and Middle Farallones a wildlife refuge in 1906. In 1969, the South Farallones Island was added. A brick lighthouse tower was placed on the South Farallon.

Human personnel operated the lighthouse until 1972 when it was replaced by an automated system. The lighthouse is considered one of the most important on the western coast as the Farallones lie in the track of vessels coming from the westward to San Francisco.

The wind blows fiercely most of the time and the ocean current is rough.

One of the numerous caves worn into the rocks by the surf had a hole at the top. When the incoming breakers crashed into the cave, air was violently expelled.

Engineers were able to devise a trumpet or fog-whistle, with the mouthpiece fixed against the aperture in the rock. When a breaker came dashing in, it would blow the fog-whistle, warning mariners off, as a bulging wave could dash a ship to pieces.

Lighthouse keepers on the Farallones led a lonely, monotonous existence. While their house was built under the shelter of rocks, they lived in what to a landsman would seem a perpetual storm.

The ocean roared in their ears day and night and the boom of the surf was their constant and only music.

In the winter months, even their supply vessel, which was, for the most part, their only connection with the world, would be unable to make a landing for weeks at a time.

Few humans were ever on the Farallones, but the islands are filled with animal life. They provide a home for a multitude of sea lions and vast numbers of birds and rabbits.

The rabbits are descendants of a few pair brought to the islands many years ago in an effort to establish a huge rabbit warren that would supply the San Francisco market.

During the California gold rush, when provisions were high-priced and eggs were scarce, egg gatherers went to the Farallones. Once in 1853, a boat dispatched to the Farallones came back three days later with one thousand dozen bird eggs.

The entire cargo was sold for one dollar per dozen. An egg war ensued, and the conflicting egg seekers armed themselves and became so violent the government of the United States was forced to step in to keep the peace.

Chapter 22

'A Hand To Bank On'

There is a story told throughout the west where gambling played a part of the cowboy's and gold miner's life.

According to one version, the cashier for a Denver bank arrived to open up one morning and found three weary-looking men sitting on the steps.

"Want to make a deposit, gentlemen?" he asked. "Step inside."

"No, I want to negotiate a loan," replied one of the men, "and there ain't a minute to lose. I want $5,000 quicker than hell can scorch a feather."

He explained that he and the others were involved in a poker game at the saloon across the street. There was $4,000 already in the pot, and he needed a loan to stay in the game.

As collateral, he proffered a sealed envelope containing his "hand"—the cards he was holding in the poker game.

When the cashier opened the envelope, he found four kings and an ace, an unbeatable hand by the rules of the day in western gambling houses, before the advent of straight flushes and royal flushes. The cashier turned the loan applicant down.

Back on the street, the disappointed gambler ran into the bank president. The president took one look at the gambler's hand and dashed inside the bank. He grabbed a bag of $20 bills and followed the trio back to their game.

Ten minutes later, the banker returned to the bank, and tossed the original bag of money and an extra handful of 20s for interest, onto the counter.

The banker then gave the cashier a lecture on the nature of collateral.

"Remember, that in the future four kings and an ace are always good in this institution for our entire assets, sir—our entire assets."

Chapter 23

The 'No-good' Utica Mine

John Selkirk was ready to call it quits. He'd groveled in the dirt of his worthless claim long enough and only needed enough money to go back home to Massachusetts.

Selkirk silently rode his mule through the slovenly little gold camp called Angels Camp looking straight ahead. At a bushy place on a hillside just beyond the last shanty, Selkirk unpacked his blankets, his pick, shovel and pan from the back of the saddle, and threw them carelessly on the ground.

He built a fire and put his coffee on to boil and fixed a quick supper. He then lay idly, smoking his pipe and thinking of home.

"I'll light out of here in a few hours and go back to the folks," Selkirk told himself.

A noisy jay interrupted his reverie. The jay screamed from the brush, scolding Selkirk for usurping his territory.

Looking for something to throw at the jay, he looked around and found a small gray stone. Selkirk's eye caught the glint of yellow embedded in the stone.

Selkirk broke the stone into fragments, and the pieces were heavy with gold.

He grabbed his hand axe and cut some sticks from a nearby oak tree. These he drove into the ground at the four corners of a rectangular piece of hillside containing fifteen to twenty acres.

Selkirk had just staked the Utica Mine, the richest gold deposit in California.

He worked hard during the following days, finding little ore on some days and more on others. His crude *arrastra*, worked by mule power, and his other primitive mining methods for crushing the hard rock and extracting the gold from it, brought him very little in the way of shiny gold bars.

Selkirk knew he had a rich mine, but he needed better mining methods. He went to Sacramento and to Benicia, laying his case before men of wealth.

He went back to his mine without the funds he needed. While Selkirk was pecking away down inside his mine, a prospecting party came along, peeked down into the hole where the sweat-stained Selkirk was working.

"What have you got down there?" one man asked.

"Biggest thing in the world," Selkirk replied, as he climbed the ladder to the bright sunshine.

"Want to sell?"

"Yes, I would sell, if I could get my price."

"What is your price?"

Selkirk replied, "I'm sick and worn out, and if you'll give me two hundred dollars to get home on I'll let you have it."

Miners descend the shaft at the Utica Mine.
(Photos reprinted from "Tales of California"

This is how its original discoverer sold the great Utica Mine.

Even the first buyers did not exploit the mine to its potential, and slowly, one by one, each partner dropped out to go looking for a rainbow.

The mine was then abandoned. It became overgrown with weeds and other miners dismantled the twenty-stamp mill.

James G. Fair heard the stories of the rich diggings in Angels Camp. Riding a stage to the site, Fair hired a guide to show him around.

When he peered into Selkirk's old hole-in-the-ground, he asked the guide, "What's down there?"

"Nothing but water," replied the guide. "But there's a good property back on the hill I want to show you."

"But I'm going to see this first," Fair said. He removed his coat and prepared to descend the ladder.

"It's old and rotten," warned the guide. Still, Fair lowered himself halfway down the shaft and into a drift to which the water had not reached.

He picked up several pieces of quartz that the last workers had chipped loose. These he brought up into the sunlight. As he did so, he drew the attention of curious idlers.

"What could anybody want down in Selkirk's old hole?" they wondered.

Fair, however, like the looks of the quartz, but said nothing. Soon afterward, he had an expert miner sift carefully through the drifts of the old

Selkirk mine. A few weeks later, equipment was at work bailing out the stagnant water in the hole.

Fair set up a mill, put men to work underground to delve and drift along the vein. He also put men to work cutting and hauling timber to hold up the walls of the shaft.

Soon Fair saw a stream of gold begin to pour out of the mine—gold enough, indeed to pay and feed all hands, keep the machinery in repair and see a new surplus come in every month.

Fair knew that the Utica was a mine of magnificent prospects, but he also knew that it was baffling, rebellious and expensive.

He soon began investing in mines on the great Comstock ledge in Nevada and in other properties and he became wealthy. He abandoned the Utica to take care of itself. It was a rich mine that nobody wanted.

In 1880, Charles D. Lane bought the Utica Mine for $10,000. He was warned that he was pouring his money down the proverbial rat hole, and his friends considered him as becoming demented.

Lane himself worked hard in the mine in an attempt to develop the Utica. He exhausted every dollar of his resources, along with another fifteen thousand he borrowed. His credit was now exhausted along with his resources.

It was at this time that another figure appeared in Angels Camp. This was Alvinza Hayward, considered one of the shrewdest of the old time mining men of the Coast.

Lane intended to interest Hayward in his Utica Mine. Hayward took a few samples of the quartz from the Utica back to San Francisco. It was a long while before Lane hard from him.

Finally, Lane and Hayward dickered over an arrangement to work the Utica. Lane wanted Hayward to advance him money enough to pay his debts and enable him to get back to work. He suggested that $30,000 would do it.

Hayward, however, did not have that much capital. But he did induce a third man, named W.S. Hobart, to join the group.

Lane surrendered two thirds of the Utica property, and retained one-third for himself. Lane paid his debts, increased the work force at the mine, and within a few months a report echoed through Angels Camp that the Utica Mine had struck a rich find.

Hundreds of men were put to work at the Utica. The latest in stamp mill design was installed along with other machinery to work the tailings and getting the last drop of gold from the earth.

The Utica became the greatest gold mine on the Pacific Coast and was considered one of the wonders of California.

Chapter 24

Salting A Gold Claim

It wasn't unusual for the owner of a worthless gold claim to "salt" it to make it more valuable.

Salting a gold claim involved sprinkling gold dust about in certain places in the mine to make it appear richer than it was. The practice became so common that purchasers were advised to be on their guard.

In 1851, a party of American miners was working a claim near the little town of Columbia, in Tuolumne County. When they did not strike any color from their hard work digging, the miners became discouraged.

A group of Chinese miners working nearby expressed some interest in the mine. The Americans extolled the richness of their mine and put a high price on it.

The Chinese were dubious. The Americans invited the Chinese miners to bring their own picks and pans and prospect for themselves. The miner's, believing it would be their last chance to sell, decided to "salt" the claim.

It was a large claim. The problem for the miners was where to put the salt. Then, one of the men hit upon an ingenious plan. He went out with his gun and shot a rattlesnake.

He told his partners, "Now, when the *Chinamen* come tomorrow, they won't allow any of us to be too near, because they're afraid of 'salt'. Well, Jim, you put the dead snake in your pocket and walk along the bank, while Bill and me stay talking to the *Chinamen.*"

"I'll have my gun over my shoulder as though I'm going to hunt rabbits. I'll load it with gold dust. When they indicate where they want to pan next, you slide that snake down the bank. When them fellows start to walk there, I'll holler, 'Hold on, boys!' I'll fire the salt at the dead snake, making believe I had killed it."

When the Chinese indicated where they wished to inspect, the man holding the dead snake was signaled to throw the snake there.

The game went as planned, "Hold on boys," the American said, and walked to the snake, firing into the ground where it lay, "salting" the ground beneath it. With the barrel of his gun, he hoisted the snake. The Chinese buyers had no suspicion of what had happened.

When the Chinese miners carried several pans of dirt away to wash in a nearby stream, the Americans were sure they had found the salt. Still the Chinese miners said only, "Claim no good. "Melican man talkee to muchee."

The American's knew the game the Chinese played and refused to take less than the specified price. The Chinese bought the mine in two days.

It may have been the American's that came up losers on the deal, as the mine became one of the richest in the district. The Chinese made a great deal of money working the mine, then sold out and returned to China.

Webster Had the Answer

When Daniel Webster was a young man on the farm, he had trouble with his scythe. It would not "hang" right.

After fixing it two or three times, his father told him to "hang it to suit yourself."

Young Daniel hung it on the fence and left the field.

Chapter 25

John Colter:
'His Wild Escape from the Indians'

John Colter's encounter with Blackfoot Indian warriors proved beyond a doubt that he was indeed a mountain man.

The Indians chased him naked for six miles across the cactus-strewn prairie.
(American Vision Organization)

Coulter and another man named John Potts were trapping beaver on the Missouri River. To be sure, they were encroaching on Blackfoot hunting grounds, but the beaver were so plentiful that Colter and Potts couldn't make themselves leave the bountiful area.

Early one morning, when the two trappers paddled their canoe to gather pelts from traps they had placed the night before, they heard trampling on the riverbank. "Indians," Colter said, wanting to turn back.

Potts thought the sound was made by buffalo, and kept on paddling.

They soon were surrounded on both shores by hundreds of Blackfoot warriors. The Indians made clear signs for the trappers to come to them.

As they got to shore, one Indian grabbed Potts' rifle. Colter, a big man, wrested it back and handed it to Potts, who made the mistake of killing an Indian with it. Potts' body was shot full of arrows.

The Indians now took Colter, stripped him, and talked of how they would kill him. At first, they were simply going to put him up as a target for the Indians to shoot at.

Colter could understand enough of their language to know what they were saying. The Indian chief thought it would be greater sport if they gave Colter the chance to run.

He asked Colter if he could run fast. Colter, who was indeed a swift runner, lied, saying he was a poor runner.

The chief took him out on the prairie a few hundred yards and turned him loose to run for his life. The Indians, giving a war-whoop, hurried after him.

Colter ran straight across and open plain toward the Jefferson River, six miles away. The plain was covered with cactus, and with every leap Colter's bare feet picked up more thorns.

Still, Colter ran faster than he had ever run in his life. He was halfway across the plain before he ever looked back. When he dared look back over his shoulder, he saw he had outrun all of the Indians except one. This warrior carried a spear and was not more than one hundred yards behind him.

Blood gushed from Colter's nose and covered his body. Still, he ran on until within a mile of the river, the Indian behind closed in. Colter stopped, turned around and spread out his arms.

The Indian, exhausted also, tried to stop but instead fell to the ground, breaking his spear. Colter grabbed the point of the spear and plunged it into the Indian.

Colter then ran on, while the other Indians came up to their dead comrade. Colter soon gained the shelter of the trees on the bank of the river, and plunged into the stream.

Downstream was an island with a giant raft of driftwood floating on the water. Colter dived under the raft and found breathing room by sticking his head between two large logs supporting the raft.

The trapper no sooner hid himself beneath the raft than the Indians came down the bank, yelling like fiends. They hunted for him along the shore and even walked out on the raft over Colter's head.

Colter waited until after dark, when he could no longer hear the Indians, to venture from his hiding place. He swam down the stream a long distance before climbing ashore.

He was alone in the wilderness, without a weapon, and his feet were torn to shreds from their encounter with the cactus thorns. He was several

143

hundred miles from the nearest trading post on the Yellowstone, in a country of hostile savages.

He reached the trading post 11 days later, sunburned and starving, but alive.

His continued encounters with the Blackfoot Indians eventually drove Colter to give up trapping. With his proceeds from the pelts he had gathered, he moved to New Haven, Missouri, and in 1810, married a woman named Sallie.

When the United States declared war on Great Britain in 1812, Colter enlisted. He fought under Nathan Boone. It was in the service that he died, not from fighting the British, nor from the hands of the Blackfoot Indians. He died of jaundice.

His body was shipped back to his wife Sallie in Missouri. Sallie was unable to provide a proper burial, so his body was left lying in state in the cabin. Sallie moved to her brother's home.

John Colter's body continued to lie in the cabin for the next 114 years, the house slowly disintegrating around him. In 1926, the land on which the cabin stood was being cleared. During the process, Colter's bones, along with a leather pouch bearing his name, were found.

His remains were gathered and buried on a bluff in New Haven, overlooking the Missouri River.

(The above story was taken from an account written by Addison Erwin Sheldon in 1913. Sheldon was director of the Nebraska Historical Society.)

Chapter 25

Slavery in Early Oregon

While the Oregon Provisional Government declared slavery illegal in Oregon in 1844, it was done for the wrong reason.

The ban on slavery had nothing to do with abolitionist leanings. It was just the opposite. Slavery was outlawed in Oregon as a means of keeping the black population in Oregon to a minimum.

Owning slaves was tolerated in the Northwest, and some slaves successfully sued for their freedom or the freedom of loved ones. No whites were ever forced to free their slaves upon entering Oregon Country after 1844.

Some whites did free their slaves, however, and a small population of free blacks became established in the Pacific Northwest. Slaves were too valuable for owners to want to give them up.

Racism became widespread and severe along the West Coast in the years leading up to the Civil War. The California legislature came close to passing exclusion laws twice, prompting many free blacks to head for the British Columbia. Some slaves still held in the old Oregon Country escaped north as well.

Pro-slavery groups agitated repeatedly to form a new federal territory—and eventually a new slave state—out of what is now southwestern Oregon and northern California.

Such plans failed as California refused to cede any of its land.

Oregon's early racial politics were dominated by a wish to simply be free of the problem altogether by not allowing blacks to settle there.

When it enacted a provision to make slavery illegal in 1844, the Provisional Government of Oregon said that settlers who owned slaves would have to free them within three years. Any free blacks, 18 or older, had to leave the area. Men had to leave within two years, and women within three.

The original Oregon exclusion law was the infamous "Lash Law" which subjected blacks found guilty of violating the law to whippings. It was recognized that this law was too severe and it was modified before it went into effect.

A new version of the law replaced whippings with forced labor. This law was repealed in the 1845 session of the Provisional Legislature.

Exclusion laws had been prominent in other states, including Missouri, Illinois, Indiana, and Ohio. All four states denied blacks the right to vote and restricted their ability to testify in court.

Chapter 26

Mormons and Crickets

A plague of grasshoppers attacked the first wheat crop in Utah in 1848. The Mormons, newly arrived in the state, planted the crop.

It appeared that all was lost for the pioneers who had just settled the territory. Then, when the worst was feared, a white cloud of seagulls flew in and devoured the locusts.

Locusts were everywhere.
(Google Images)

This story was repeated many times in the diaries kept by the pioneers. The story became a faith-promoting tale that was told and retold.

There is a seagull monument on Temple Square that is said to be the only monument in honor of the seagull. As was appropriate, Utah has recognized the seagull as its state bird.

Even though the seagull rescued Utah's first crop of grain, future generations have not always been so lucky. Grasshopper invasions became a common experience in pioneer Utah.

The insects approached the state in a swarm that could be seen from a long distance. *The Deseret News* reported one massive appearance in which "the grasshoppers filled the sky for three miles deep, or as far as they could be seen without the aid of a telescopes."

The locusts would fly overhead for several hours a day for a period of two or three weeks.

Minerva Edmerica Richards Knowlton recalled the locusts gave off a noonday buzzing and seemed like the sun going behind a cloud. Also, she said, something bumped against windows and doors. When she went outdoors, she found millions of the Rocky Mountain locusts all over the house, garden, and yard. She recorded in her diary:

"The family washing had been put out early that morning, and the 'tobacco juice", as the children called it, stained the clothing so badly that the home-made soap and boiling the clothes on the kitchen stove each washing, never fully removed the stains."

Sometimes the locusts refused to leave, even in inclement weather.

Benjamin LeBaron recalled the year 1868 when it rained. The locusts would gather on the trunks of trees, on fence posts and every other object that might afford them some shelter.

In 1877, The Deseret News described a confrontation between grasshoppers and railroad traffic. The paper wrote:

> *The destroying insects are abroad! They are coming this way. They are armed and legged and winged—as orthodox angels should be—and fully equipped for war. Their maneuvers are not exactly according to the manual, but they act in concert and their march is irresistible. On the sand ridge between this city and Ogden, they are out on parade. But the engine of the U.S. passenger train this morning dashed through their ranks with defiant snorts, and countless numbers were done to death.*

Chapter 27

Susan LaFlesche Picotte

Daughter of Omaha Indian
Chief Joseph LaFlesche (Iron
Eyes), Susan LaFlesche Picotte
was the first Native American
woman to earn a medical degree.

She was born on the Omaha
reservation in Nebraska and
attended school there until she
was fourteen years old.

Susan LaFlesche
Picotte.
(Google Images)

When she attended
Women's Medical College in
Philadelphia, she graduated at the top of her class
and became the first Native American woman
physician.

Following graduation, Dr. LaFlesche returned to
the Omaha Reservation and worked as a physician
for the government school. She fought a widespread
cholera outbreak, dysentery, and influenza diseases
as a doctor on the Reservation.

As a child on the prairie, Susan helped with
family chores. She followed her father often,
learning from him all things from herding the
tribe's animals to the wisdom he departed to other
tribesmen.

Her father wanted Susan and all the tribe's children to be educated and to know their way around the white men's world.

Susan watched the white doctor as he ministered to the Indians on the Reservation. Sometimes she noticed how slow he was, and at other times, the obvious uncaring in his handling of patients.

She wondered often how she could best help her people. In 1879, Susan and her sister, Marguerite, traveled to the Elizabeth Institute for Young Ladies in New Jersey. They studied there until 1882.

While Susan tended to Alice Fletcher, an ill anthropologist, she began to wonder if she could learn the skills necessary to help people medically.

In 1884, she left to study at the Hampton Institute in Virginia. There, she met the school doctor, Dr. Martha M. Waldron. With her aid, she entered Women's Medical College in Philadelphia in 1886.

It pleased Susan when all Omahas became United States citizens in 1887. She completed her studies in 1889 and returned home.

She made her home and office at the Omaha Agency School in Macy, Nebraska. From there, she not only doctored—on horseback, and later a buggy—she worked fifteen-hour days, helping her people through cultural changes.

She resigned as the government doctor in 1893 and moved to Bancroft, Nebraska where she opened a private practice, treating both Native and non-Native Americans. A year later, she married Henry Picotte. They had two sons, Caryl and

Pierre. Her husband, however, died of alcoholism, a problem on the rise on most reservations.

Susan moved with her sons back to Macy. Her dream for a hospital on the Reservation came true in January 1913 when the Dr. Susan Picotte Memorial Hospital was completed at Walthill, Nebraska.

As a member of the State Medical Association, Susan worked to combat alcoholism among the Omaha, and she lectured in favor of temperance. Her work brought about a stipulation that every property deed in communities on the Omaha reservation would prohibit the sale of alcohol.

The hospital that was named in her honor existed until the late 1940s. Later, it served as a care center for the elderly. In 1989, the building was restored and it now displays photos and artifacts from Dr. Picotte's life.

Her father, Chief Joseph LaFlesche had great foresight. Not only Susan but the other LaFlesche children were well-educated, learning the culture of two worlds, that of the Omaha tribe and that of the white population in which they had to live.

Chapter 28

The Spindletop Oil Find

It was just a small hill south of Beaumont, Texas, but it opened up what is considered today the modern oil industry.

Patillo Higgins was a one-armed mechanic and a self-taught geologist. He had a gut-wrenching certainty that he knew where great quantities of oil lay, waiting to be brought to the surface.

Higgins was having trouble convincing his business partners to commit to his proposed venture. They thought his ideas were impossible and ridiculous.

Higgins finally convinced his backers to hire a drilling crew. The drawback was that drilling technology was still inadequate for what Higgins proposed.

Luckily, Higgins was able to find another man, Capt. Anthony F. Lucas that believed as much in the hill as Higgins did.

Lucas was an experienced mining engineer. At first, he met with many of the same problems that Higgins had dealt with. By the late 1900s, his personal funds were almost depleted.

But Lucas had been able to secure the services of capable drilling contractors, the Hamill Brothers of Corsicana, Texas.

The discovery of oil at Spindletop in Beaumont, Texas in 1901 triggered an oil rush reminiscent of the Gold Rush. A forest of derricks sprang up along Spindletop's Boiler Avenue. Speculators divided and sold land tracts as small as one-thirty-second of an acre to drillers.

(American Petroleum Institute)

On the morning of January 10, 1901, the hill south of Beaumont began to tremble and mud bubbled over the rotary table. A low rumbling sound came from underground. Then with great force, six tons of four-inch metal pipe was shot over the top of the derrick, the Lucas Gusher roared at Spindletop.

A six-inch stream of green-black oil spouted more than 100-feet over the top of the derrick. Estimates say that as much as 100,000 barrels a day was spilled by the spewing oil well.

This one well was producing more oil that all the other oil wells in the United States combined.

Captain Lucas served in the Austrian Navy and had training as an engineer and as a salt miner in Louisiana.

Native American Indians were aware of the oil seeps for centuries. They used the tar they found at the surface to treat a variety of ailments. Some even drank the black goo in hopes it would cure digestive problems.

In 1543, Spanish explorers discovered the sticky tar that washed up on the beaches of the Texas coast could be used to waterproof their boots.

The first deep wells drilled in the area were in search of water, and the oil that seeped up in the drilling process was an annoying nuisance. Well drills pushed past these oil zones in order to get to the water they wanted.

Drilling was difficult at first. Lucas and his men ran into the same problems that other drillers had faced along the Texas plain. There is little in the way of rock at the surface in that part of the world.

Instead, wildcatters had to drill through several hundred feet of sand, making the hole prone to caving in on the workers. Curt Hamill, one of Lucas' drillers came up with a solution to this problem.

Instead of pumping water down the hole to flush out the cuttings produced by the drill action, Hamill suggested using mud. The mud proved to help in retrieving the cuttings and also helped in shoring up the sides of the hole.

Mud has been used in almost every drill hole around the world since that time.

On January 10, 1901, the drilling crew began lowering back into their hole. They had the drill to a depth of about 700 feet when all of a sudden, a noise like a cannon came from the hole.

Within a few seconds, an oil gusher rose to more than 150 feet high. Captain Lucas had hoped for a mere five barrels of oil per day from the well. It turned out to flow at 100,000 barrels per day.

The area where Spindletop is located was very different 150 years ago than is appears today. At that time, it was part of a shallow sea that would occasionally dry up, leaving tons of salt. In time, great thicknesses of salt accumulated.

Salt is a funny kind of rock. If lots of pressure is put upon it, it begins to move. It's movement is upward toward the surface because its density is less than surrounding rocks.

Broken rocks can act as a very effective trap for oil and natural gas.

Another method of trapping oil occurs at the top of the salt dome in a zone called cap-rock. Nearly all salt domes along the Gulf Coast have a disk-like cap-rock, composed of minerals such as gypsum, anhydrite, limestone, sulphur and dolomite.

There are cavernous spaces that form in this zone, forming miniature caves that fill with oil. When an oil drill penetrates this zone, the oil comes out of the ground fast and furious.

Spindletop changed the way that oil exploration took place.

Chapter 29

Oklahoma Land Rush

It was 1889 and the federal government was opening a choice portion of Indian Territory in Oklahoma up to settlers. Two million acres of Oklahoma Territory was being put up for grabs.

At noon on Monday, April 22, 1889, Guthrie Station in Oklahoma was almost nothing. Before sundown, it had at least ten thousand people.

Congress failed to provide for any form of civil government for the big land rush. Never before in the history of the west had so large a number of people been concentrated in one place in so short a time.

A lot of preparations had been made. The Santa Fe Railroad, for instance, was prepared to take any number of people from its station at Arkansas City, Kansas, and deposit them at almost any part of Oklahoma as soon as the law allowed.

People of all classes of society hungered for that little place of their own. There were impoverished farmers, tradesmen, professional men, common laborers, capitalists and politicians in line to stake their claim.

The NewYork Herald observed that "...men will fight harder for $500 worth of land than they will for $10,000 in money."

Hordes of people converged on entry offices to qualify for the great Oklahoma Land Rush. (Google Images)

The Unassigned Lands were left vacant in the post-Civil War effort to create reservations for Plains Indians and other tribes. These lands were considered the best-unoccupied land in the nation.

In 1889, would-be settlers massed in camps at the Kansas border towns, especially at Arkansas City and Caldwell. U.S. troops were on hand to restrain the eager crowd.

As the hour for the opening approached, great crowds waited on the border, while mounted soldiers stood guard to turn back intruders.

At the stroke of noon, starting signals were given at the many starting points. No matter what starting point it was, the pistol shot of the starter produced a tumultuous avalanche of wagons and horsemen, all surging forward in one breathtaking instant.

Sometimes, when a husband made his wild dash to choose his 160 acres, he would hear a rousing cheer from his family that remained behind on the sidelines.

When a home seeker found a tract of land he liked, he drove a stake into the ground to mark his possession and held it as best he could against other claimants.

Merchants brought merchandise in their wagons to start a store in a new town. Stores opened in the backs of wagons, then moved to a tent a day or two later until a building could be erected.

Eight land-rush trains left Arkansas City, each loaded to the maximum with anxious contestants.

There was an estimated eleven thousand homesteads claimed. Some would be contested in the days ahead for one reason or another, but it was a significant day in national history.

Schools opened in tents the week following the great land rush. Volunteers were paid by the pupils' parents until the cities and counties could establish regular school districts. The law provided for land in each township be reserved for school use.

The weeks following the big land rush were busy ones for the newcomers to the frontier. Within a month, Oklahoma City had five banks and six newspapers. Greengrocers were doing a thriving business. Fresh tomatoes sold for 15 cents a bushel and eggs were three cents per dozen.

Even though the settlers were without any organized government for a thirteen-month period, good order prevailed. Frontier living conditions were too rigorous and money was too scarce to attract outlaws.

The big Oklahoma Land Run of 1889 set the stage for non-Indian settlement of other sections of Indian Territory. It led to the creation of Oklahoma Territory under the Organic Act of 1890 and ultimately to formation of the forty-sixth state of the Union.

Oklahoma was admitted to the union as a state in 1907.

Chapter 30

The Range Wars

The bitter conflict between cattlemen and sheepmen covered nearly five decades in which more than fifty humans and some fifty-three-thousand sheep were killed.

This conflict began in Texas and Colorado but spread to other territories where cattlemen objected to the entry of sheep onto their ranges.

Most cowboys disliked the sheepherders as much as their bosses did. A cowboy that was sympathetic to the sheepmen was called a *"sheep dipper."*

As the cattle ranges in Texas became overstocked in the 1880s, violence increased between the sheepmen and cattlemen. When the arctic winter of 1886-87 caused cattle to die by the thousands, the open range way of doing business pretty much ended.

Cattlemen realized that if they wanted to succeed, they had to be in both the land business as well as the cattle business. Consequently, competition for the remaining public domain became intense. Cattle ranchers, small stockmen, homesteaders, and sheepmen all vied for the properties available.

The number of sheep increased slowly but steadily across the west. Simple economic reality favored sheep ranching. Sheep produced two products, wool and mutton, and both could produced more economically than beef. Sheep could subsist on range that would not support cattle. A sheep could live on sagebrush and sparse upland grasses and they required a third less water than cattle needed.

Another factor was that investment in a sheep operation was considerably less than that for an efficient cattle operation.

Wool being hauled to market in Texas
(Texas State Archives, Austin)

One of the men who realized the benefits of sheep ranching was Bryant B. Brooks, a pioneer Wyoming cattle rancher who was also the state's governor from 1905 to 1911.

According to Bill O'Neal, in his book, "Cattlemen vs. Sheepherders", Brooks soon discovered that sheep brought year-round jobs to

Wyoming and a steadier measure of prosperity than other agricultural enterprises.

Brooks decided that he too would enter the sheep business. He bought a band of three thousand sheep in Denver. The band had not been shorn nor had they yet lambed. Brooks realized a handsome profit, which encouraged him to invest more heavily in sheep.

Another thing that came home to Brooks was the fact that sheep were less injurious to the range than were cattle. "Cattle graze over the same range all the year and feed differently from sheep, invariably eating the coarser, taller grasses first, thereby destroying the seed stalks so the ranges do not reseed. Sheep eat the flowers, weeds, and fine grass first, and let the stalks alone."

Many cattlemen, however, refused to have anything to do with the detested sheep, and some of them were so adamant as to wage war against the sheepmen.

These attacks were usually aimed at isolated sheep camps. The attackers were mounted cowboys who often wore masks, sometimes made of gunnysacks. *Gunnysackers* became a common name for these marauders.

While most of the sheep were shot, there were times when the animals were clubbed with ax handles or wagon wheel spokes. Some of the sheep did not die outright but had their backs broken or were otherwise maimed.

This photo shows sheep that were clubbed to death near Tie Siding, Wyoming.
(American Heritage Center, University of Wyoming, Laramie)

In Colorado, sheepmen were quick to rebel when a cattlemen's organization in Pueblo County announced that sheep would have to be confined to certain ranges.

The sheepmen fought back with their own strong statement:

> "If you have not already learned you are now made to understand that wool and mutton are as necessary as 'beef and broad brimmed hats and revolvers.'"

The statement of the sheepmen was ignored, for when sheep rancher A.D. Robinson brought twenty four hundred head of sheep into Las Animas County, adjacent to Pueblo and Huerfano counties, eight or ten men struck, killing and wounding a considerable number.

War after war was reported throughout the range country where cattlemen and sheepmen were pitted against each other.

It was in Wyoming where cattlemen put up their strongest defense to keep sheep from taking over their ranges. The Wyoming Stock Growers Association commanded a powerful position in territorial affairs. The WSGA had an annual budget of $52,796, compared to the entire territorial budget of $38,000.

Battlegrounds in Wyoming included courtrooms as well as rangelands. There was a brief lull in the range war when entire herds of cattle were left dead during the arctic winter of 1886-87.

Many of the ranchers were forced out of business, leaving a devastated Wyoming Stock Growers Association. Its membership dropped from four hundred sixteen members in 1886 to just sixty-eight members in 1890.

Sheep ranchers quickly filled the void left by the devastation of cattle by the freezing winter. Some cattlemen also decided they would be better off raising sheep than they would cattle.

By 1900, the Wyoming Stock Growers Association was revived and again cattlemen became a force in the state. They again resisted the sheepmen and "nesters" that were occupying good rangeland. Stockmen also suspected that some of the cattle being raised by the farmers came from their herds.

The cattlemen decided to take strong action against rustlers of their cattle. One incident concerned Emma Watson, known as "Cattle Kate."

Kate ran a bawdy house, and was known to trade her favors for rustled cattle. Her partner, Jim Averell, was brought to trial for shooting a ranch foreman in the leg.

Cattle Kate and Averell were warned to leave the county, and in addition a rustling charge was lodged against Averell. The two were hanged from a tree on July 20, 1889.

Convictions of seven men in Wyoming for the murder of five sheepherders on April 2, 1909 pretty much brought a close to the cattlemen-sheepmen wars. There were later scattered events, but by the 1920s, both sides stopped using vigilante methods to solve range rights.

Stockmen, both growers of sheep and of cattle, resorted to their state legislators to bring order to the range.

Chapter 31

The Night Riders

> These mysterious riders wore their white hoods to protect their identity. They rode their horses at night, burning crops, tearing out railroad ties, and harassing people.

They were called *Las Gorras Blancas* (The White Caps)..

The White Caps were vigilantes of San Miguel County, New Mexico, who fought furiously against any changes that came upon their land. The group was comprised mainly of native shepherds and farmers, who viewed the railroads as their enemy and not as a symbol of prosperity.

Anglos began buying land. They built fences to establish the fact that the land was indeed private property. This meant that neighbors could no longer graze their animals in these communal pastures.

Communities such as Sapello, one of several small towns in San Miguel County located along the Santa Fe Trail, couldn't cope with the rapid changes taking place. The coming of the railroad was causing them to lose their land, forcing them into unwanted career changes.

Before the railroad, Sapello's lifeline was the Santa Fe Trail. The Trail provided convenience in travel and in trade. People traveling through Sapello on their way to Mora County, Las Vegas and Santa Fe often stopped in Sapello and spent their money.

Las Gorras Blancas decided to restore the old ways by cutting fences and stopping the railroad.

These mysterious riders wore their white hoods to protect their identity. They rode their horses at night, burning crops, tearing out railroad ties, and harassing people.

Behind their masks, Las Gorras Blancas threatened with death anyone who associated with their hated target, the railroad. The nightriders made their mark by fence cutting, and eventually caused as much as twenty-seven thousand dollars worth of fence damage in 1880 alone.

They rode into the town of East Las Vegas, New Mexico just before midnight, March 11, 1890, two hundred riders strong. They paraded silently through the streets, crossed over the Gallinas River Bridge into West Las Vegas where they paused in front of the home of Sheriff Lorenzo Lopez.

They then moved on to the San Miguel County Courthouse and then to the jail, where they sat silently for a while before disappearing into the darkness.

Los Gorras Blancas had made such nocturnal visits before, but this time they scattered printed circulars explaining their fight against those who were appropriating and fencing tracts of common lands for their own use.

171

This photo shows Las Vegas Plaza in the 1880s after the coming of the Santa Fe Railroad. (Museum of New Mexico)

No one questioned that Los Gorras Blancas meant business. Appearing on horseback under cover of darkness, the White Caps tore down miles of wire fencing and fence posts, burned barns and haystacks and scattered livestock.

The cause of the turmoil was confusion over the status of the Las Vegas Community Land Grant. This grant was surveyed in 1860, with a resulting measure of 496,444.96 acres.

In 1835, the Mexican government had set aside the lands surrounding Las Vegas, New Mexico and within the grant boundaries, to be held in joint ownership by the original Las Vegas colonists and their heirs and successors. These lands were to be an undivided community and open for grazing, hunting and wood gathering.

U.S. officials, however, insisted that the common lands had become a part of the U.S. public domain, eligible for private settlement and development.

Anglos bought up and fenced tracts of land, moved livestock onto them, planted crops and diverted water from streams to irrigate. This put Hispanic farmers and ranchers who depended on these lands for their livelihood out in the cold.

The people of Las Vegas sympathized with the White Cap movement, but outside of Las Vegas, the image of the vigilante group was not so good. They were pictured as anti-Anglo terrorists and outlaws who were giving New Mexico a bad name.

In their circulars, the White Caps explained their positions, which were printed by a number of New Mexico newspapers:

Our Platform
Not wishing to be misunderstood, we hereby make this our declaration:

Our purpose is to protect the rights and interests of the people in general, and especially those of the helpless classes.

We want the Las Vegas grant settled to the interest of all concerned, and this we hold is the entire community within the grant.

We want no "land grabbers" or obstructionists of any sort to interfere.

173

We will watch them. We are not down on lawyers as a class, but the usual knavery and unfair treatment of the people must be stopped.

The position paper continued at length, and was signed by the White Caps, with the notation:
"1,500 Strong and Gaining Daily".

The White Caps continued with their raids and even extended them into adjoining Santa Fe and Mora counties.

Pablo Herrera, a former prison inmate, was elected to the New Mexico Territorial Legislature in the 1890 elections.

He sat quietly through several sessions of the Territorial Assembly in Santa Fe before deciding he had had enough. At the close of the legislative session, Herrera rose from his seat and delivered this brief address to his colleagues:

"Gentlemen, I have served several years time in the penitentiary but only sixty days in the Legislature, the present House of Representatives.

I have watched the proceedings here carefully.

I would like to say that the time I spent in the penitentiary was more enjoyable than the time I spent here.

There is more honesty in the halls of the territorial prison than in the halls of the Legislature.

I would prefer another term in prison than another election to the House."

His political career thus ended, a short time later Herrera was convicted of third degree murder in the stabbing death of Doroteo Sandoval in a West Las Vegas saloon.

A friendly jailor allowed Herrera to escape and a two hundred dollar reward was offered for his arrest. A sheriff's posse on a West Las Vegas street shot him to death on Christmas Eve, 1894.

By the time of Herrera's death, the White Cap raids in San Miguel County had ceased as there were no fences remaining on the common lands and no new ones were being built.

The land-grant matter was resolved in 1903 when the Town of Las Vegas was given ownership of the disputed lands and a board of trustees was established to administer them.

Chapter 32

The Ride of His Life

Aubry rode hard, covering one hundred miles a day. When he arrived in Independence fourteen days later, he had beat the record set by Norris Colburn in 1846 by ten and a half days.

He was called "Little Aubry" and weighed perhaps one hundred pounds soaking wet. But he could ride!

As an adult, Francis X. Aubry stood only five feet two inches tall.

After traveling to St. Louis, Missouri, traders assured him there was a lot of money to be made in transporting and selling trade goods in Santa Fe, New Mexico.

Francis X. Aubry
(Kansas State Historical Society)

The diminutive Aubry secured a loan from a St. Louis firm and hired a freighting firm to transport the goods to Santa Fe. When he arrived, he found that Santa Fe was now in American hands. When Mexico attacked American troops on the southern border of Texas, General Winfield Scott occupied Mexico City and ended the war.

The U.S. annexed Texas and Mexico ceded California and New Mexico, including all the present-day states of the southwest.

Aubry sold his goods for enough money to pay off his debt. He then became involved in carrying the U.S. Mail, as well as transporting goods over the Santa Fe Trail from Missouri to Santa Fe.

Government and military mail was taking at least thirty days by mule. When sent by ox teams pulling heavy freight wagons, it took sixty to ninety days.

He offered to carry the mail on a return trip from Santa Fe to Independence, Missouri, which he was making by horseback. He left Santa Fe December 22, 1847 with a party of four men and a servant. When Mexican bandits attacked the party, everybody dropped out, leaving Aubry alone. Later, he lost another ten hours fighting off some Indians.

Aubry rode hard, covering one hundred miles a day. When he arrived in Independence fourteen days later, he had beat the record set by Norris Colburn in 1846 by ten and a half days.

Little Aubry wasn't satisfied. He was sure he could make the ride in eight days.

Bettors lined up to place their money on Little Aubry's wild ride. Aubry, himself, bet one thousand dollars that he could beat his previous record. In fact, he bet that he could complete the ride from Santa Fe to Independence within six days.

He was better prepared for this ride. He sent men ahead with fresh horses and had then stationed all along his route.

He left Santa Fe at a full gallop for the ride of his life on September 12, 1848. He changed horses at various stops along the way. When he neared Point Reyes early in the morning. His favorite mare, "Dolly" was waiting for him.

Even in the rain, this small mare of Spanish blood didn't slow down. He rode Dolly one hundred miles before he planned to get a new mount. As he approach the station where he would change horses, instead of a new mount, he found a dead man that had been scalped by Indians.

The Indians had also run off the horses. He would ride Dolly another one hundred miles before finding a wagon train with horses.

Dolly had set a record, traveling two hundred miles at a speed of eight miles an hour over a twenty-six hour period.

At ten o'clock at night September 17, Little Aubry pulled up in front of the Merchant's Hotel in Independence. He was weak but alive. Men rushed out to help him from the saddle.

He had won his bet, making the ride from Santa Fe to Independence in five days and sixteen hours.

In 1853, fortune played a cruel trip on the little rider. This event occurred in 1853 when Aubry was taking ten wagons filled with merchandise from Santa Fe to the gold fields of California.

Aubry kept a meticulous diary of his trips. On August 3, 1853 he wrote:

Indians shooting arrows around us all day wounded some of our mules and my famous mare, Dolly, who has so often rescued me from danger by her speed and capacity for endurance.

On August 16, after being wounded eight times, and he and his men were on half rations of horsemeat, Aubry added another entry to his diary:

I have the misfortune to know that the flesh we are eating is that of my inestimable mare Dolly who so often saved me from death at the hands of Indians. She gave out on account of her wounds.

A year later, Little Aubry himself was stabbed to death while at a *cantina* in Santa Fe.

Index

windmills, 79, 80
Wyatt Earp, 27, 28, 29, 30
Wyoming, 166, 167, 168,
169, 170

Yellowstone National
Park, 73
YUBAN, 63
Zebulon M. Pike, 105

Meet the Author

Alton Pryor has been a writer for magazines, newspapers, and wire services since 1954. He worked for United Press International in their Sacramento Bureau, handling both printed press as well as radio news.

Alton Pryor

He moved to Salinas, where he worked for the Salinas Californian daily newspaper for five years as editor of Western Ranch and Home, a weekend supplement.

In 1963, he joined California Farmer magazine where he was a staff writer for 27 years. When that magazine sold, the magazine's writers were let go. Alton then pursued freelancing, and gained an intense interest in California and Western history after selling ten short 500-word articles on Southern California history.

While researching these topics, he found other stories that interested him but did not fit the publication for whom he wrote. He collected the facts and ideas as he researched, and finally turned them into his first book, "Little Known Tales in California History."

He is a graduate of California State Polytechnic University, San Luis Obispo, where he earned a Bachelor of Science degree in journalism.